As mom to four childre
ago to keep growing a.
long to become the moi
I love books that inspii
*Growing Great Kids* is just such a book. It's packed
with powerful stories, teaching, and everyday life
application. Thanks, Kate, for sharing your journey.
May we all learn to love our kids and see their hearts
with the same tenderness, wisdom, and grace.

—ANGELA THOMAS
BEST-SELLING AUTHOR AND SPEAKER

Unlock the greatness within your child—regardless
of age. *Growing Great Kids* will inspire and equip
you with biblical principles and practical insights
as a Christian parent. This is a great parenting
resource and pragmatic guide. Read it now and see
great results immediately in your parenting and your
child's maturity.

—DR. LARRY KEEFAUVER
INTERNATIONAL TEACHER AND AUTHOR
OF *THE 77 IRREFUTABLE TRUTHS OF PARENTING*
AND *LORD, I WISH MY TEENAGER WOULD*
*TALK WITH ME*

Someone once told me that if you see a turtle on a
fence post, it did not get there by itself. It got there
because someone helped it. The Battistellis will be
quick to tell you that God is the one who has given
Franny so much success. I totally agree and He did
much of it through the day-in and day-out work of
her parents, Mike and Kate.

In her book, *Growing Great Kids*, Kate Battistelli unwraps some of the most godly, practical, wise, and honest parenting insights I've ever read. My wife and I have already merged many of her steps into our parenting strategy, and as a result we feel more confident about growing great kids. Every parent needs to absorb this book!

—Tony Nolan
Author and Minister

Parents need to have a vision for the big picture of their kids' lives in light of God's Word. Without this vision, many parents, along with their offspring, are wandering aimlessly.

Kate's book helps give parents the "big picture." Character, integrity, finding the way a child is bent, all are so important, and Kate expresses these big ideas in such a warm, easy way! Ron and I had a great time reading this together and found the questions and prayers at the end of each chapter especially helpful in bringing the points right home to where we all live. I've read plenty of child-rearing books in my days of raising four boys, and I only wish this one was around then. I'll make sure they and their wives each have a copy of this book!

—Sandy and Ron Johnson
Lead Pastors, Markham Woods Church

Kate Battistelli takes the reader on a humbling and honest journey of raising a child in today's world. Through each page she'll make you smile and she'll make you think, and all the while, Battistelli prayerfully opens up your own heart to dream large for your children, to truly grow great kids. A wonderful and faith-filled read!

—STACIE A. VINING
PUBLICIST AND COOWNER OF MERGE PR

*Growing Great Kids* is a practical and powerful testament to the wisdom and truth Kate and Mike applied to their parenting of their remarkable daughter. Who in this world will dream bigger for children than their parents? Who will sacrifice more? Guard their hearts and minds? As the father of two boys who have very different personalities and possess great potential in very different areas, this book serves as a great encouragement and reminder to me of the power and responsibility of parenthood.

—MICHAEL BIANCHI
CHANNEL/PRODUCT DIRECTOR,
WORLD VISION ARTISTS

I am honored to be a wife and mother, a gift I cherish. Kate Battistelli's book is a gift to us all! I am grateful for Kate's pearls of wisdom and her beautiful heart that radiates in the joy of parenting. I believe *Growing Great Kids* will be an inspiration to all who have the privilege of raising God's children! Proverbs 22:6 says, "Train up a child in the way he should go, and when he is old he will not depart from it." Mike and Kate, you have done just that, and now we have a book to train us all!

—SHELLY BALLESTERO
AUTHOR OF *BEAUTY BY GOD*

Kate Battistelli doesn't pull any punches. Do you want your kids to drift through life, or do you want them to make a splash for God? Because, says Kate, it's really up to you. In a world where too many drift through the parenting years, parenting by default, Kate urges us on to greatness, for it's only as our children use their God-given gifts and talents that we can fight back against our dark culture. Kate isn't in the blame game; she's in the inspiration game. She's trying to inspire us to reach for the moon when it comes to parenting our kids, because our culture desperately needs godly, successful kids. I find her candor refreshing. She's actually telling it like it is. She's not sugarcoating it. And we need that, because too many of us are parenting wimps. What she's saying is that God made you a parent—so act like it. Embrace it. Do it excellently! That is why God put you in your child's life.

—SHEILA WRAY GREGOIRE
MARRIAGE AND PARENTING COACH AND
AUTHOR OF *TO LOVE, HONOR AND VACUUM*

# *Growing* GREAT KIDS

# Kate Battistelli

CHARISMA
HOUSE

Most CHARISMA HOUSE BOOK GROUP products are available at special quantity discounts for bulk purchase for sales promotions, premiums, fund-raising, and educational needs. For details, write Charisma House Book Group, 600 Rinehart Road, Lake Mary, Florida 32746, or telephone (407) 333-0600.

GROWING GREAT KIDS by Kate Battistelli
Published by Charisma House
Charisma Media/Charisma House Book Group
600 Rinehart Road
Lake Mary, Florida 32746
www.charismahouse.com

Cover design by Bill Johnson
Cover photos: Tim Kelly Portraits

Visit the author's website at www.katebattistelli.com.

Library of Congress Cataloging-in-Publication Data:
An application to register this book for cataloging has been submitted to the Library of Congress.
International Standard Book Number: 978-1-61638-654-2

E-book ISBN: 978-1-61638-655-9

First Edition

12 13 14 15 16 — 987654321
Printed in the United States of America

To my amazing husband, Michael: For all the years we've been together, you have always supported, encouraged, loved, and believed in me. We jumped into this parenting journey together, and with God's help we raised a great kid. I love you with everything in me, and I'm so glad you are my puzzle part.

To my daughter, Francesca: I consider it an honor to have had the opportunity to raise you, and I stand in awe of the woman of God you have become. I love you more than words can say. You are my heart, forever and always.

*The father of the righteous will greatly rejoice, and he who begets a wise child will delight in him...and let her who bore you rejoice.*

PROVERBS 23:24–25

# CONTENTS

# ACKNOWLEDGMENTS

T HANK YOU, Joy and Steve Strang. I'm grateful you've given me the opportunity to take the message of *Growing Great Kids* to the world.

To Diana Scimone, writer and writing coach extraordinaire! You gave shape and structure to my idea and made me believe I could actually write a book. Thank you for encouraging me and helping me to dream big!

To Maureen Eha, for your friendship, encouragement, and patience to answer my thousand and one questions. And, more importantly, for believing in what I had to say and convincing me others would find it worth reading.

To Jim and Linda Werner: thank you for asking Mike and me to speak at the Circle Christian School twenty-fifth anniversary celebration. As we prepared for our talk, the notes we took turned into chapter headings that ultimately became *Growing Great Kids*. God planted a seed that night to speak to my heart and show me the book that was living inside.

To the talented team at Charisma House: thank you for all your hard work, help, and patience working with a new author. A special thank-you to my editor, Jevon Bolden, as well as Design Director Bill Johnson, Marketing Director Woodley Auguste, and Marketing Coordinator Jihan Watkins.

A huge thank-you to photographer Tim Kelly for his fabulous photos on the front and back cover.

To Jenny Fox Shain, life coach: When this book was just a thought with no shape or direction, your words of encouragement in the lobby of a church in Georgia lit a flame and helped me believe that other parents would embrace the principles learned along our parenting journey.

To my friends who contributed stories: thank you for your wisdom and insights. You have all grown great kids, and I'm blessed by your willingness and transparency to share your parenting journey with me.

To God, my Father: "O LORD, You are the portion of my inheritance and my cup. You maintain my lot. The lines have fallen for me in pleasant places. Yes, I have a good inheritance. I will bless the LORD who has given me counsel; my heart also instructs me in the night seasons. I have set the LORD always before me. Because He is at my right hand I shall not be moved" (Ps. 16:5–8).

# FOREWORD

MANY PEOPLE ASK me what it was like growing up as an only child (as if I'm the only human on the planet who has experienced this phenomenon). Specifically they ask if I felt like I "missed out" on anything. I'm sure there were times I was envious of my friends with siblings because it seemed like they had built-in playmates, little brothers to torment, and so on. But for the most part, I truly relished being an only child. I was so close with my parents, and I had such a big imagination, that I actually enjoyed all the time I had to myself.

I was blessed to have a dad who worked from home, a mom who homeschooled me, and a childhood full of some remarkable experiences. Whether it was getting to be involved in professional theater from the age of twelve on, taking hours and hours of ballet classes (my first love), going on trips to some incredible cities and countries around the world, going to ministry events with my mom, or learning how to cook from the world's greatest chef (also my mom), I have many memories from those years that I cherish. Life in those days felt like one giant adventure. You'll read about some of those adventures in this book—even the embarrassing ones—and you'll learn from the wisdom and experience of my very favorite woman in the whole wide world.

My mom has poured so much of her heart and life into this

book, and you will definitely reap the benefits of all of her hard work. I pray that you will be inspired, encouraged, challenged, and moved by what you read, and I pray that your paradigm will change for the better after reading this book. As a brand-new mom myself, I have already learned so much from it.

Growing great kids is a lifelong journey that will take humility, courage, and good old-fashioned elbow grease. But it is so much easier and more rewarding if you have a relationship with Jesus. He wrote the first book on parenting (also known as the Bible), and if you don't know anything about that, then I hope you keep reading! May He bless you with abundant joy in parenting and beyond!

—FRANCESCA BATTISTELLI GOODWIN

# INTRODUCTION

P ARENTS, WE HAVE the divine gift and precious responsibility of mining and nurturing every bit of potential we
recognize in our children. To a large degree, our children's success or failure depends on how we raise them, how
we value their dreams, the work ethic we instill, and the moral
code we live by. This will all directly affect their level of success
as they grow and the degree to which they impact the world
around them.

Are there other factors involved? Of course! Intellectual
ability, temperament, character, and environment also impact
the outcome of their lives. But who else sees the budding Picasso
in the finger paint, the Beethoven in the banged out version of
"Twinkle, Twinkle, Little Star," or the mini-Einstein in the science fair volcano as we do? We have the ability to recognize and
nurture what we see in our children.

Successful adults don't happen by accident. It takes intentional effort to raise a child into an adult who has a strong sense
of their destiny in God, a passion to serve Him, and a deep
knowledge of His gifts and callings. Parents, we know our children better than anyone else. By partnering with God we can
equip them to be all He called and created them to be. It's up
to us to equip (not push or apply undue pressure) our children
to go after their dreams.

Proverbs 22:6 says, "Train up a child in the way he should go, and when he is old he will not depart from it." These treasured words teach that we have a responsibility. We have to do the training. We will see the "way they should go." God will clearly show it to us. And we will lead them in that way.

It was obvious when my daughter, Francesca, was a little girl that she had a flair for the dramatic and a bent toward the performing arts. So into ballet she went, then show choir and community theater, singing lessons, and later professional theater, guitar lessons, camps, conferences, and college—all with an eye toward the future and a sense God had a plan for her in the world of performing arts.

Did I know when she was four years old and starting ballet she would grow up to be a Grammy-nominated contemporary Christian singer with five Dove Awards and five top ten singles? Did I know her songs would be played on a variety of television shows and major motion pictures—all within the first two years of her career? No. But I knew God had something special for her—just as He has for *your* child.

As we sought God for wisdom and clarity for her call, He narrowed the field, closed some doors but opened others, and step by step made her path clear. It was a family affair and involved lots of hard work, financial sacrifice, hours upon hours of practice (and driving!), and the inevitable emotional upheaval when things didn't go exactly as planned. But looking back, the lessons learned formed her into the successful adult she is today, and there's little I would change.

Our part as parents was recognizing her particular bent—her gifts, callings, and destiny—and making the way possible for her to explore them to the full. Her part was being diligent in her work, honoring her commitments, practicing and perfecting her skills, and always giving her best and pursuing excellence. It wasn't always easy for her or us. We learned along the way it's never OK to settle for good enough.

You may be reading this and thinking, "Wow, they were the perfect parents and did everything right. No wonder their daughter turned out so well." Actually, nothing could be further from the truth! The reason I'm sharing my parenting journey with you is because I made so many mistakes along the way. I messed up plenty, and you may too. The thing is to keep moving forward, correct the things you know to correct, repent, and move on. I experienced firsthand, with many failures along the way, both sides of all the chapters you are about to read. Being a parent is a work in progress. Babies don't come home from the hospital with a how-to manual. But we have the absolute best parenting manual available, and that's the Word of God. So it's OK if you fail from time to time. Just keep going and trust the Lord and know you are growing a great kid!

But we must be diligent in our responsibility to instill purpose, destiny, and a passion for excellence in the children God gives us. We need to teach our children to honor God by being the absolute best they can be by developing the gifts they have been given: "To whom much is given, from him much will be required" (Luke 12:48). Our kids can be nothing less than world changers if we do our part and let God do His!

Raising a child to be a world changer in any field takes discipline, time, diligence, and patience. As parents, our actions greatly determine a child's ability to reach the full potential God designed for him. Join me in the pages to come as we explore how to dream God's big dream for your child, the importance of pursuing purity of heart and mind in an impure culture, learning to recognize the oak tree in the acorn, knowing how to interpret God's season in your child's life, the value of humility and integrity, the power of our words, and much more.

The journey begins!

# 1

## GIFTS AND CALLINGS

WHEN MY DAUGHTER was little, she definitely had a flair for the dramatic. She was fun-loving but with a serious side and a true sense of right and wrong. There was a Burger King commercial on television back then, and the tag line was "Sometimes you just gotta break the rules!" Each time it would come on TV, Franny would loudly shout, "No, you don't! You don't break the rules!"

She loved to sing and dance and change her outfit half a dozen times a day, and I began to have a sense that maybe my little drama queen was inclined toward the performing arts. So like millions of moms do every day, I signed her up for ballet lessons. To say she loved it would be an understatement. She took to it like a duck to water—loving the pink tights, the hair in a bun, and especially when Miss Gina would single her out for a word of encouragement!

As time went on, I started getting the sense that maybe God had something more for her in the performing arts. That's when we intentionally began to take steps to expose her to the arts in a variety of small ways such as seeing the annual production of *The Nutcracker* at Christmas, watching old movie musicals, and taking her to children's theater productions. We didn't take huge steps, but we made small investments to see how she responded and to see if my hunch was right. For her seventh birthday we took her to see the Broadway production of *The Secret Garden*, and she was completely captivated with the show and with musical theater in general from that moment on. That's when my husband and I really began praying about her future and what more we might do to help mine the treasure in her.

## MINING THE GREATNESS

Mine (noun):

1. an excavation made in the earth for the purpose of extracting ores, coal, precious stones, etc.

2. a place where such minerals may be obtained, either by excavation or by washing the soil.

3. a natural deposit of such minerals.[1]

Precious metals and precious stones are embedded in rocks and have to be extracted. Metals especially don't generally appear in nature in their pure form. Shafts and tunnels are cut into the earth. The rock is quarried and then smelted with heat to remove the dross from the ore. It's a difficult, tedious process, and it takes time and effort. The results, however, are certainly worth the effort to tap those precious veins beneath the earth. Our children's gifts are sometimes buried deep. It's up to us to mine the gift in them, extract it, and allow it to be shaped and polished to be useful in building the kingdom of God. The effort requires selfless dedication on our part and an investment of time and finances, but one that pays lifelong dividends in the life of your child.

What is God showing you about your child? What traits is he expressing? What most interests or intrigues him? Is he outgoing or introspective? Is he intellectual or athletic? Is he artistic and creative or mechanically minded and good with his hands? And what are the dreams you have inside for him? Do you have a knowing deep inside about his life? Has God given you a glimpse into his future? What do you see when you pray for him?

I believe it's my job to find out who God made my child to be. What particular path has He set for him? What's unique about his personality, gifts, talents, and aspirations? How do I help him find the life God has already planned for him? What is God's purpose for his life, and how do I train him to accomplish his purpose?

Psalm 139:13–16 says it so beautifully:

> For You formed my inward parts; You covered me in my mother's womb. I will praise You, for I am fearfully and wonderfully made; marvelous are Your works, and that my soul knows very well. My frame was not hidden from You, when I was made in secret, and skillfully wrought in the lowest parts of the earth. Your eyes saw my substance, being yet unformed. And in Your book they all were written, the days fashioned for me, when as yet there were none of them.

He knows our paths and has already written them in His book!

I don't claim to be an expert in child rearing, but I am an expert in raising *my* child. Just as you are an expert in raising your child. The fact is, no one knows your child better than you, and as your child grows and develops, his gifts and talents will be more obvious to you than to anyone else.

Train up a child in the way he should go [and in keeping with his individual gift or bent], and when he is old he will not depart from it.

—PROVERBS 22:6, AMP

Parents, we are the trainers, and *train* is an active word! We train the whole child in the Word and godliness, in faith and biblical principles. We train them to obey and honor Him in thought, word, and deed. We train them to pursue their future careers and callings. We do them a great disservice if we take this responsibility lightly. God has given us a sacred trust by allowing us to be the stewards of our children.

Here is the note on this scripture in my *Spirit-Filled Life Bible*:

> **"Train up"** has the idea of a parent graciously investing in a child whatever wisdom, love, nurture, and discipline is needed for him to become fully committed to God. It presupposes the emotional and spiritual maturity of the parent to do so. **"In the way he should go"** *is to do the training according to the unique personality, gifts, and aspirations of the child.* It also means to train the child to avoid whatever natural tendencies he might have that would prevent total commitment to God (for example, a weak will, a lack of discipline, a susceptibility to depression). Hence, the promise is that proper development insures the child will stay committed to God.[2]

There are many good resources available on how to raise your child in "the nurture and admonition of the Lord" (Eph. 6:4, KJV). I'm trying to convey something else in this book. If you are a Christian parent, it's a given that you will raise your child to love God with all his heart, soul, mind, and strength.

Teaching our children to know and love God and to delight in Him should be our highest aim as we raise our kids.

My goal is to inspire you to partner with God to mine the greatness that's lying dormant in your child. Each of us is capable of far more than we think we are. I truly believe we are capable of greatness, and we shouldn't be afraid to pursue it. God will show you the gifts and talents, the callings and destiny residing in your child. For your children to become all that God has designed them to be means you have to be willing to go the extra mile and not assume they will simply "figure it out" when they are grown.

Too many parents seem content to allow their children to drift into young adulthood and then wonder what turned them into adultolescents (a person who has physically matured to adulthood yet still behaves like an adolescent) and why they seem to have no direction in life. Childhood is an innocent time of wonder and discovery and endless possibilities, and it desperately requires our care, nurturing, and firm direction! Helping your child to explore life's endless possibilities will open the floodgates to dreaming big dreams. As time goes on, with your guidance he will narrow his choices, focus on what really interests him, and embark on the path to building a future in the center of God's will for his life.

I firmly believe God shows parents from the time their kids are small what He has invested in them. He shows us their bent, and our job is to dig deep and find the depth of the gifts and callings buried inside. It is important we are not too busy or distracted with life to see what God is eager to reveal to us in each of our children.

## Bumps Along the Road

When Franny had just turned twenty years old, she backed into a lawyer's car, in the lawyer's driveway, after the lawyer had warned her to "be careful not to back into my car." Naturally she felt foolish and was extremely upset. She knew Dad was likely to ask his famous twenty questions when she got home and was not looking forward to it. As she was driving home, she began crying and praying. The Lord began to speak to her heart, reminding her she wasn't perfect and it was OK with Him. He made her the way she was and to just relax and trust Him. She began singing this chorus: "I got a couple dents in my fender, got a couple rips in my jeans, try to fit the pieces together but perfection is my enemy. And on my own I'm so clumsy, but on Your shoulders I can see, I'm free to be me."[3]

The next day she sat on the end of her bed and played for her dad and me the finished song God had dropped in her spirit during the drive home the day before. It might sound crazy, but as soon as I heard it, I knew this was a hit song. This occurred way before Franny moved to Nashville, signed a record deal, or had any inkling anything like that was even possible. But I knew, because God knew and was just sharing my daughter's future with me. Three years later "Free to Be Me" was the first single by a female artist to hit number one at Christian radio in eight years, remaining at number one for ten weeks!

## Grammy Story

People ask me all the time, "Did you ever think your daughter would do so well?" "Did you ever think you would hear her on the radio?" or "Are you surprised by her success?" The answers are yes, yes, and no! Mike and I always had a "knowing" deep inside about her career path as she got older. We sensed where God was going, and we let Him plant big dreams in us for her.

From the time she was fifteen and beginning to pursue music more seriously, we would watch the televised Grammy Awards every year, and every year I would say to her, "You're going to be up there one day." I don't know why I said it; I just knew deep down it was true, and knowing words have creative power, I believed it important to actually speak it out.

I found an old journal recently and in thumbing through it came across this entry—February 28, 2002:

> Hi, Lord. It's me, bugging You! Last night we watched the Grammys, and Franny's emotions were so stirred she cried through much of it. Mike says I set her expectations too high, but I believe if You are going to go for something, go for the highest. It's not that it's so important to win an award, but winning represents being at a level where you have respect and acceptance. I know she is willing to work hard and she will work hard. Show her mercy and encourage her in all her hard work. Let her redouble her efforts and give it everything she's got. Show her Your favor and love. Raise her up in the music business and let her be a shining, warm, beautiful light. Give Mike and I wisdom with how to guide her. Thanks, Lord!

In December 2009, seven years after I wrote in my journal, Franny was nominated for a Grammy Award in the Best Gospel Performance category for her song "Free to Be Me"! People asked me if I was surprised, and truly I can say I wasn't. I'd been praying about it for seven years! I was thrilled of course, but not surprised. It was just one more confirmation of what I already knew. She hasn't won a Grammy yet, but I'm still praying!

## MY STORY AND I'M STICKING TO IT

Franny comes by her gifts naturally. She has the added benefit of parents who happened to stumble upon, believe in, and latch onto God's principles for growing great kids. While it is certainly an unmistakable advantage to be raised immersed in these principles, successful adults can and do spring from circumstances where these principles are absent, but perhaps at play to some degree in the background. I didn't have parents who followed these principles, yet I was able to dig down deep and define what I wanted in life and pursue it. However, I wouldn't recommend rolling the dice with your children by failing to employ every asset in your parenting arsenal to stack the deck in favor of your child's future.

I grew up in circumstances quite different from those I trumpet on these pages and yet somehow found a successful future in spite of it. My life's circumstances led me on a journey that took its inevitable detours, but it's my life story and I'm sticking to it! Just so you have a little background and can understand better where I'm coming from, here's my story.

I grew up in an encouragement vacuum. My parents had four kids, and I assumed my place tucked right in the middle at number three. I was a child of the 1950s and 1960s and the conventional worldview of parenting in quasi-Christian homes during that era, and my parents were busy with the social priorities of their all-American suburban lives.

As far as spirituality and growing up, I remember two things vividly about God. I remember being in Sunday school at maybe four or five years old and singing "Jesus loves me, this I know"[4] and completely believing it was true. Whoever Jesus was, I *knew* He loved me. The other thing I recall was thinking to myself when I was about six that I didn't ever want to die, and if there was a way to live forever, I was going to find it.

12

I grew up attending the Episcopal Church. I learned all about the life of Jesus, but I never knew Him in a personal way and I didn't know He could live in my heart. I enjoyed church. The mystery and beauty of the liturgy, the candles and Communion, the fragrant flowers, beautiful stained glass, and impressive organ music all contributed to my feeling of awe about God and awareness of my insignificance. Our church had beautiful stone floors so your footsteps echoed as you walked along. I loved the hymns we sang and the readings from the *Book of Common Prayer* and the mystery of taking Communion. I knew God was contained in all those things, but I didn't sense a clear pathway to meet Him. It was His house after all, but how did you take Him home?

To her credit, my mom had us kneel by our beds every night to say the Lord's Prayer and blessings over the family. My grandfather was a man of strong faith. He used to read Bible stories to us when we stayed over, and he would make them come alive. We would beg him for just one more! He would write in his Bible and underline scripture, something I take after him in. We could often find Grandpa stretched out over the couch in his office praying for what seemed like hours. We always knew not to disturb him during those times. He was not a perfect man by any means, but those things I witnessed in him. His love for God and his devotion to his church and family have stuck with me all these years.

My childhood was pleasant with the typical ups and downs but no major traumas or tragedies.

I rarely heard words that affirmed my value and potential or words encouraging me to believe the world was my oyster and I could be anything I wanted to be. There were lots of arguments between my parents and all the siblings. Expectations were high of course, but there was precious little praise and encouragement to attain them and far too much criticism. Somewhere in

13

adolescence my self-esteem began to suffer, and I no longer felt comfortable sharing openly with my parents. My future lacked any kind of shape with no real direction. I didn't have a clear-cut path to run on with lots of support and nurturing. So I floated through high school. I floated through four colleges in two years. I was adrift with no focus and no goals.

I knew from the time I was a little girl that I loved to sing. It was my one passion, and I did what I could to develop my singing in high school. I joined the choir and did the yearly high school musical. We happened to have a wonderful and dedicated voice teacher at my high school, so I took advantage of her lessons. But I was pretty much on my own in my pursuit of music.

I asked my mom years later why she never pushed me or encouraged me in music, and her response was fairly typical for her generation. She felt if it was really something I wanted to do, I'd pull myself up by my own initiative and make it happen. Actually, she was right. It's exactly what I did, but I think I would have avoided a great many pitfalls along the way if I'd had her support.

As it happened, I discovered musical theater when I turned twenty. I began working in a local community theater where I lived in New Jersey and in two years performed in more than fifteen productions. I got a crash course in musical theater to say the least! I stumbled on an article in a magazine about goal setting, and because it made logical sense to me, I started setting some practical goals. Not long after, I was auditioning for roles in New York City. I got my Actors' Equity card and started doing lots of regional theater, actually surviving as a working actor—barely.

I began working with an agent, and he secured me an audition for the Broadway national tour of *The King and I* starring Yul Brynner. My audition was for the role of the understudy for the part of "Anna," played by Deborah Kerr in the movie. I was a young actress in my twenties, and this was by far the biggest thing that had come along for me. To make a long story short, I got the role of the understudy and happily packed my steamer trunk and went out on the road. I faithfully rehearsed my part, never thinking I would ever really get the chance to perform. But when preparation meets opportunity, miracles can happen!

## Life Comes at You Fast

About two months into the run of the show, I arrived at the theater around 7:15 p.m. for the 8:00 p.m. curtain, only to find out the leading lady was sick and I was going on for the first time as the leading lady in forty-five minutes! I knew my part well but had never worn the costumes or handled the props, let alone been onstage with Yul Brynner! I was freaking out, but I had to focus and get ready. The night turned out well, and I got to perform the role of Anna for two weeks while the leading lady was out with pneumonia. In the end, Yul Brynner (who not only starred in the show but was also one of its producers) preferred me in the role, so he bought out the leading lady's contract and offered me the role of a lifetime! It was an amazing time for me. I was privileged to play the part of Anna more than a thousand times, before more than a million theatergoers, over the next two and a half years!

The best part of the entire experience, though, was meeting my husband, Mike. He joined the tour about six months into the run of the show as the associate conductor, and as he likes to say, we literally fell in love across the footlights!

After performing eight shows a week for the next two and a half years, we left the tour, moved back to New York City, got married, bought a little condo in Greenwich Village, and began our new life together. A year later we found ourselves answering an altar call and giving our hearts to the Lord. Franny was born a year later, and we thoroughly enjoyed our new little family amid all the excitement of living and working in the hustle and bustle of New York's music and theater world.

It wasn't long, though, before we began to feel the tug on our hearts to lay down the business we had worked so hard to find our way in and follow what God had in store for us next. Bucking conventional wisdom but following what we believed was God's best for our family, we eventually left New York and our careers behind to embark on building a new life that included moving to the suburbs, starting a new business, and homeschooling our little girl.

## MEET MY HUSBAND, MIKE

Mike comes from a family without a rich musical heritage. In his case, however, his parents were very encouraging and supported his early interest in music. They purchased the finest musical instruments they could afford, drove him to weekly trumpet lessons at the Juilliard School preparatory division, and sacrificed to send him to National Music Camp in Interlochen, Michigan, during the summer. He later graduated from Interlochen Arts Academy, received his bachelor's degree from the Eastman School of Music, and went on to earn his master's and doctorate in music. He was a studio musician and played trumpet and flugelhorn in Broadway pit orchestras and musically directed and conducted on Broadway, on national tour, and at Radio City Music Hall. In his case, he was the first in his family who expressed any gifting in music. Often children inherit their parents' gifts and carry on the family business, and other times they plow new ground.

With both her parents involved in musical theater professionally, you could say Francesca was destined to go into the arts, and specifically music. It was more likely in her case because of the very musical environment in which she was raised, not to mention being thrown into the deep end of her parent's gene pool! But not every child's course is as easy to recognize.

With our daughter, obviously she inherited gifts and talent in music and the performing arts. Our job was to take those gifts and give them shape, give her opportunities to be trained in those areas, and expose her to teachers, classes, and mentors who would take her where God called her to go. We couldn't assume she was going to follow exactly in our footsteps. And we had to make sure she knew her gifts and talents weren't what defined her. We were going to love her no matter what life she chose. We had to seek God for His wisdom in her unique expression of her gifts in the performing arts. Our part was to mine those gifts and talents, and her part was to be diligent with what God entrusted to her. Success doesn't happen by accident. It takes years of hard work.

I believe if we seek Him, God is faithful to put a dream in parents' hearts for their children. He gives us a sense as they grow. Sometimes it's just an inkling that turns into a knowing and over time becomes a certainty. He entrusts the dream to us and gives us the responsibility to dig it out and give it shape. Kids don't become successful adults by accident.

## SUCCESS AND ENVIRONMENT

In Malcolm Gladwell's *Outliers*, he writes:

> People don't rise from nothing. We do owe something to parentage and patronage. The people who stand before kings may look like they did it all by themselves. But in fact they are invariably the beneficiaries of hidden advantages and extraordinary

opportunities and cultural legacies that allow them to learn and work hard and make sense of the world in ways others cannot. It makes a difference where and when we grew up. The culture we belong to and the legacies passed down by our forebears shape the patterns of our achievement in ways we cannot begin to imagine. It's not enough to ask what successful people are like, in other words. It is only by asking where they are from that we can unravel the logic behind who succeeds and who doesn't.[5]

The first place your child is from is you. You will have the biggest impact on his future. How you live, how you love, how you handle money, what you do in your free time, and the standard of integrity and honesty you set in your life—all these things and many more will shape your child into the adult he will become. You alone can give him the "hidden advantages and extraordinary opportunities," and as you seek the Lord, He'll show them to you.

How many families do you know whose adult children can't seem to commit to their own future? And parents who don't have a clue as to how to guide them? There is a culture of drift all around us—adults with no goals or dreams who are living out their lives in mediocre jobs, having little impact on society. If parents abdicate their responsibility and give it over to the school system or the church, they contribute to the drift. We aren't supposed to be going nowhere. Destiny connotes a destination. But God won't do it for you. You have to do it in partnership with God.

Who you are is going to shape who your child becomes. If education is important to you, you will raise your child expecting him to go to college and get good grades, barring any serious learning disabilities. If learning to manage money is important in your family, then you will teach your child about budgeting at an early age and require him to earn the money to buy the things he wants and get a job when he is old enough. If parents are extravagant in their spending, their kids will be too! If sports are important in your family, you will set an example by making exercise a priority and being available to coach your child and take him to games and sporting events. If the arts are your passion, you will expose him to great music, museums, ballet, and theatrical productions. If you believe there is greatness in your child, you will find it and find ways to mine it!

## IT'S ALL IN THE NAME

When Franny was a preteen, I became curious about what her name meant. I knew that *Battistelli* meant "to hit the stars," and I wondered what the name *Francesca* meant. So I looked it up at the bookstore in one of those baby name books. I found out the name *Francesca* means "free." I was *stunned*! It was one more confirmation of what I was beginning to sense about her future, and I excitedly told her and Mike what I'd found. Her name meant "free to hit the stars." Talk about a prophetic picture! I was able to encourage her and remind her during down times just what her name meant and the destiny it conveyed.

## PERSONALITY—WHO IS SHE LIKE?

One thing that fascinated me when my daughter was young was the difference in our personalities. I'm pretty steady emotionally, calm, cool, and very practical and unsentimental. I love home, family, and the homemaking arts such as cooking, gardening, and so on. My husband is more of a type-A personality. He is a leader, strong-willed, and independent with a strong work ethic and a dedication to personal integrity. Our daughter isn't exactly like either of us. She is sensitive, emotional, analytical, introverted, and a bit of a perfectionist. She has pieces of both of us but not a full distillation of either mom or dad.

God gave her a unique personality, and our job was to parent who she *was*, not who we may have wanted her to be. Also, we had to be mindful not to superimpose our unfulfilled dreams onto her life. Remember, we had achieved a measure of success in the music and musical theater worlds. It would have been easy to assume she would follow in our footsteps and go into the theater in order to fill up some leftover longing or regret in us. Actually, in our case, knowing what we knew about that world, we purposely tried to steer her away from "the business" early on and focus her on dance. However, by the time she was eleven, she was already involved in professional theater here in Orlando, Florida. She even got mom to be in several shows with her! Often the acorn doesn't fall far from the tree!

If your children are young, then now is the time to really be seeking God about their future. It's never too early to begin; in fact, the earlier the better! You probably already have an idea what their gifts and talents are. Ask God to give you a glimpse into their future. He will lead you step by step as you seek His wisdom in raising your unique child.

There is so much more in our children than we realize, and they are capable of far more than we give them credit for. There are precious metals and rare jewels deep inside your child. You will have to dig them out, but it will be well worth it when you launch them out into life knowing you did everything you could to equip them for success. And by success I mean doing what God has called them to do with passion and purpose and with Christ at the center. Perhaps God will call them into full-time ministry as a missionary. Maybe He'll give them a platform in Christian music to influence other young people to pursue God with passion and purity. Maybe your child is called to be a political leader, teacher, business owner, or inventor of something that will change the world. Maybe your daughter wants more than anything to grow up and be a mom, a noble and worthy goal. Whatever God shows you, believe it and get moving. Nothing is more exciting than partnering with God!

## QUESTIONS TO ASK YOURSELF

1. Has God given you a dream deep inside for your child?

2. What gifts and talents is your child expressing?

3. What has God put in your heart about your child's future?

4. What personality traits have you observed?

5. What practical steps can you take to train your child, both in godly principles and in helping him achieve his dreams?

6. Are you being proactive about your child's future, or are you letting him drift?

7. Do you believe that greatness resides in your child?

## PRAYER

*Lord, I come humbly before You with wonder and amazement at the precious gift of my child that You have entrusted to me. The course of his life is in Your hands, and I ask for wisdom and discernment in raising him. Help me to uncover all the gifts, talents, and callings You have placed deep inside him. I know my child is fearfully and wonderfully made, and I am excited to discover all You created him to be. Help me to be the parent he needs me to be and to have the ability to equip him to fulfill every dream in Your heart for him. Give me eyes to see and ears to hear as I raise him. Help me to be an example of integrity, humility, honesty, and diligence in all that I do. I pray this in Jesus's name!*

# 2

# THE POWER OF A
# PARENT'S WORDS

IMAGINE A YOUNG girl who loves singing more than anything in the world and she's home alone after school. In the family room she is listening to her albums and happily singing along with her beloved Broadway shows. She sings song after song from *Funny Girl* to *My Fair Lady*, imagining what it would be like to be a leading lady on the stage. Every fiber of her being is wrapped up in the music, and she is joyfully singing her heart out! Suddenly she shuts off the music because she hears the back door open, signaling that her family is home. She doesn't want to make the mistake she's made so many times before and hear the comments and critical remarks. If she doesn't turn the music off in time, they'll start yelling at her to shut up and stop making a racket. They know she can sing, but they seem to delight in teasing her and denigrating her dreams. At school people tell her she has a good voice, and her voice teacher seems to think she has a future in music, but at home, she meets a brick wall.

I wish I could say what you just read is fiction, but it reflects my life as a teenage girl. Every day when I would come home from school, as long as no one was home, I would sing for the sheer joy of it! But my passion for music wasn't appreciated and was certainly never promoted by my family. Their words stung my soul and stunted my spirit. I don't know how my future might have been different had I been given the support, praise, and encouragement I longed for. I might have actually stayed in college and gotten a degree in music!

## Words Have Power

One thing I know for sure: words have power! What you say to a person can absolutely determine his or her future. Proverbs 18:21 says, "Death and life are in the power of the tongue, and those who love it will eat its fruit." This has become a life scripture for my husband and me. Because I know firsthand the destructive power of critical words, I decided early on with my daughter that words would build up not tear down. From the time she was able to understand, I told her she was beautiful, smart, talented, a world changer, and able to be all God called her to be.

When she was small, we tried a little experiment with her. We'd lost a key in the front yard, and we honestly couldn't find it. We searched everywhere to no avail. Franny really wanted to help us, so we told her, "Go ahead and look. You are a really good finder." Well, she helped us look for a while, and wouldn't you know it, she found the key! She was so excited and we were thrilled! Anytime anything got lost, we reinforced what a good finder she was, and more often than not, she would find the lost item. In this small way we set her up in a pattern of belief about herself, and it became a self-fulfilling prophecy.

Children look up to their parents. We are the supreme authority in their little lives, and they will believe whatever we tell them. Especially when they are little, what we say carries great weight and will form the foundation of how they think about themselves.

"Sticks and stones may break my bones, but words will never hurt me." I don't know of any saying more untrue! Words have tremendous power to hurt or heal, tear down, or build up. Did you ever notice how the Bible tells us God created the universe? With a word. "God *said*, 'Let there be light'; and there was light" (Gen. 1:3, emphasis added). The entire universe burst into being with a single word from God! How eye-opening and humbling at the same time!

The way we speak to our children impacts who they are. Children hear everything we say, and they take what we say as the absolute truth. Positive, encouraging words of affirmation lovingly spoken can set a firm foundation for a child and enable her to grow into a secure adult, unafraid to pursue her dreams and goals. Critical and harsh words damage the very core of who a child is. Toxic words can poison a person's future and stunt her destiny. She grows up believing she is stupid, lazy, fat, and so on. Ladybird Johnson said, "Children are likely to live up to what you believe of them,"[1] and I would add, what you say about them. What are your words telling your child about your belief in her? Do you believe she can change the world? Then tell her!

What do your words say about your child? Are you speaking life or death to her dreams, desires, talents, and gifts? Belittling and teasing her or building her up? If God created the universe with a word, does it make sense then to believe there is creative power in our words as well? "Even so the tongue is a little member and boasts great things. See how great a forest a little fire kindles!" (James 3:5). It's a "little member," but its power to influence others for good or for evil is far greater than its small size!

## WORDS ARE FREE

You may be a mom or a dad who is struggling to make ends meet and may be frustrated you can't provide all the tools you want to help your child pursue her gifts. Words cost nothing, but they can change everything! It's easy to greatly influence her belief in herself, her belief in her gifts, and her belief in her future. Praise often! Encourage her uniqueness. Remind her God knows her and called her before the foundation of the world. He has a great plan and a great purpose for her life. Many world changers came from humble beginnings!

Some parents are under a dangerous misconception and think reverse psychology will work on their kids. Telling your child she is stupid will not motivate her to study hard. Telling her she is clumsy won't make her want to try out for sports. Telling her she is fat won't make her want to go to the gym. Proverbs 15:4 says, "A wholesome tongue is a tree of life, but perverseness in it breaks the spirit." *Wholesome*, from the Hebrew word *marpe'*, means "curative," literally "a medicine," or "cure, healing, remedy, sound, wholesome."[2] And *perverseness* comes from the word *celeph*,[3] which means "distortion and viciousness," and comes from the root word *calaph*[4] meaning, "wrench, to subvert, overthrow, pervert." So if I'm correct, you could translate it, "A healing, sound tongue is a tree of life, but viciousness in it overthrows and breaks the spirit." A child's spirit is a very fragile thing, delicate and created by God. Speaking wholesome and healing words at all times should be our goal.

I thought for years I was stupid because I was constantly told those words. Everything was, "Don't be stupid, Kate," or "Use your brain, dummy"—not very encouraging for a young person. For years I believed I really was stupid, I couldn't learn, and that intellectual pursuits were beyond my capability. I did well enough in school, but I was never consistent and I had no motivation to do well. It wasn't until I was deep into adult-hood that the Lord cured me of such an unfortunate misunder-standing about myself. But I heard those comments replaying in my head for decades, like bad eighties music!

My friend Adrianne, a devoted mother of a son and a daughter, shares her insight into the power of a parent's words:

> I grew up with a critical father and was determined even as a little girl that I would always try to find what is good in someone instead of what is wrong. From the time our children were born, my hus-band and I had to learn that our two children, even though they were born of the same parents, had very different personalities, but one thing was common—they would thrive in a home where criticism had no place. We spoke the Word over the kids, believing our words had power. I heard a pastor say one time, "If you could see your words come to life as they came out of your mouth, what you would say, and just as importantly, what wouldn't you say?" We took that to heart and spoke words of life, joy, and peace into their lives. It takes more effort to find and say what is right than what is wrong, but the payoff in the life of that child is worth every bit of the effort.

What a word picture! How powerful to imagine your words coming to life as you say them! I think if more of us did this, we would be extremely careful with what we say.

## THE DANGER IN COMPARING

Be cautious when comparing your child to siblings, friends, and role models. Saying to a child, "Why can't you be like your brother?", denies the uniqueness of the child. God made her who she is, and part of a parent's job is to dig deep and find what qualities make her special. Comparing your child to others risks making her feel inferior and believing she can never measure up to those standards.

I will always remember being compared to the "perfect" daughter of my mother's best friend. She was so smart, she had such good manners, and she was so well behaved. Why couldn't I be more like her? Unfortunately, this had the opposite effect of what was intended, and I ended up resenting her and going the exact opposite way with my life. I couldn't find affirmation at home, so I sought it out by getting involved with the wrong crowd and a dating relationship way too early. I didn't believe I could ever be as good as she was, so I gave up trying.

If you have more than one child, I pray you require them to speak kindly to one another. It should be unacceptable in your household for them to mock or criticize or put each other down. They will model what they see, so if the parents use words building up and encouraging family members, so will the siblings. Set a standard of godly speech in your household. There should be a zero tolerance policy for denigrating talk. And this goes for talk between you and your spouse. What you say to each other and about each other speaks volumes to children.

## Speak Well of Your Spouse

Our children model what they see and hear. My friend Rick, father of a son, speaks candidly about his own upbringing and the negative words he heard:

> I have always believed in the power of words and the effect that they can have on everyone around us. As believers, we are to be a positive influence and are called to be encouragers of anyone we encounter.

This especially applies to our children. I felt it was important for me to speak positive words into our son's life, but I continually fought the negativity I think molded my own personality, confidence level, and ultimately the man I became. It negatively affects a person when you continually point out their flaws, weakness, and failures instead of their strengths and gifting. It diminishes the gift of God in a life when you don't build on those characteristics and you focus on failures.

Because of my own experiences in life, I felt it was important for my son to hear me speak positively about everything, including his mother. This may seem like a small thing, but it was a strong conviction of mine. I wanted him to know exactly how I feel about his mother and the blessing that she is to my life. I told him how much she loved him and how blessed he was to have her as his mother. I told him he was so fortunate to have the best mom in the world! He still feels that way and really honors her as a grown man today.

When I grew up, it was normal for me to hear many men speak harshly toward and negatively about their wives. I never embraced this, and it always bothered me because I knew the women they were speaking of and they all seemed wonderful to me, especially my own mother. I will never forget the day, as an adult, when my father came and asked me to forgive him for the way he spoke about my mother and to reassure me about how much he loves her. He has proven this incredibly since that day.

When we raise our children, we are not just teaching them how to function in this world or how to walk with integrity. We are also teaching our children how to love their future wives, their future children, and how to interact in the most important relationships they will ever have.

What a wonderful example of the power of building up your spouse in your child's eyes!

## SAY WHAT YOU SEE

I always believed it was essential to say to Franny what I saw. As God showed me things and gave me a sense of her calling, I began to speak it out over her. Mike and I have always encouraged her in everything she's done. We always told her she was an excellent student, she was smart and talented, she had a beautiful voice, she was a great songwriter, and so on. We also continually emphasized God had a great plan and destiny for her life. Now, as she and her husband are new parents to a beautiful little boy, I tell her she is a great mom. God has shown it to me, and I know it's true!

I felt it so important when she was a young girl to remind her that she had a powerful destiny in the Lord and she was born for such a time as this. I also affirmed she was a world changer. I truly believed those things, and I knew in my heart they were right even when I didn't know what shape they were going to take. The fruit of it is, she believed it! She *is* a world changer.

Her future is limited only by God, and He is limitless.

The same is true of *your* child. Every child on this planet has a divine future and unique destiny. As God begins to show it to you, speak it out over your child. Say what you see! At night when you are praying with her, while driving her to soccer practice, around the kitchen table, always be speaking words of affirmation and possibility to her. Decree and declare destiny and success over her life. There is great power in a parent's blessing. And if she knows you believe it, she'll believe it too!

## QUESTIONS TO ASK YOURSELF

1. Examine the words you speak to your child. Are they building her up or tearing her down? Are they speaking life or death?

2. What are some ways you can affirm your child each day?

3. Are you using reverse psychology on your kids?

4. How are the siblings communicating in your home?

5. What kinds of words do your children hear you use when speaking to or about your spouse?

## PRAYER

*Lord, I decree and declare destiny over my child(ren). I declare they are blessed and highly favored, they are growing according to how You created them, and every gift and calling You put into them is developing according to Your plan. I know life and death are in the power of the tongue. I ask You to set a guard over my mouth and keep watch over the doors of my lips. Let the words of my mouth and the meditation of my heart be acceptable in Your sight. Let criticism be far from me, and help me to insure brothers and sisters, mother and father speak kindly to one another. Let all unwholesome speech be far from me. In Jesus's name, amen.*

# SEEING THE OAK TREE
# IN THE ACORN

EVERY SEPTEMBER, DISNEY World in Orlando holds a big two-day Christian music festival called Night of Joy where the top Christian recording artists come together to perform and minister. It's a great opportunity to see many of your favorite artists in one place for the price of one ticket. Because we live in Orlando, Franny used to go with her church youth group, and I would always say to her, "You know, you'll be performing up on that big stage one day."

You might know the city of Nashville is not only the center of the country music universe, but it is also ground zero for Christian music. When we visited Nashville for the first time, about three years before Franny moved there, I had a strong sense her destiny was somehow tied to the city. This was in spite of having very few contacts in the Christian music industry and no solid plan for how she might break into the world of Christian contemporary music. But I knew what I sensed about her talent in music, and the feeling I had about Nashville wouldn't go away. I would remind her from time to time that one day she was going to live, work, and thrive there. I'd also talk to her about how exciting it would be to hear her songs on the radio. I saw the future long before it came to pass, and what I saw I said as encouragement to her because I was well aware of the power of words. Since then, she's moved to Nashville, performed at Night of Joy, and had five hit songs on the radio— two of them number ones!

God shows us the gifts in our children, and our job is to speak what we see. The little acorn is there, we just have to see the oak tree. It's critical to keep encouraging them especially during the difficult years, the seasons when it doesn't seem like much is happening and they are just spinning their wheels. See the potential in them, remind them of their destiny, and know that with diligence and hard work, their dreams will come to pass.

## DREAM BIG

I've always been a person with the capacity to dream big for others. If you tell me you are thinking of studying medicine, my mind goes to the furthest limit of what's possible. What about becoming a surgeon or a researcher who is going to discover a major cure? If you're a talented athlete, why not dream big and think Olympics or the major leagues. Maybe you're a talented pianist. Why not strive for Carnegie Hall? I was talking to a young woman recently who's an anchor at a local TV station. I asked her if she'd ever thought about going national. I was unaware she had been holding on to that exact dream since she was a little girl but had received very little encouragement to believe for it. I really felt like it was possible for her, so I encouraged her to dream big and committed to pray for her.

Wouldn't you know, within a matter of weeks, she had a nationally recognized agent excited about her talent who was able to get her auditions for the major networks. I simply joined my faith with hers and spoke what I saw for her future.

It amazes me what believing for someone's future can do! I'm convinced most of us dream too small. Maybe because I was able to achieve something life changing early in my career (like starring opposite Yul Brynner in *The King and I*) it's given me a capacity for belief in the impossible and an ability to dream big. Someone is going to be the next Bill Gates—why not your child? Someone is going to discover a cure for cancer—who says it can't be your daughter?

It's a good thing to set the expectations high for your child, but do it with discernment. God will show you where He wants to take them. Your job is to call "things that are not as though they were" (Rom. 4:17, NIV) and not doubt God. Set the expectations high! We hear it preached all the time we're capable of greatness and have a big destiny in God, yet how many of us really believe it? "How can it be true of *my* kids?" you say to yourself. It *is* true, and because it's hard, it's the road less traveled. Anything worth doing is worth doing well. In sports vernacular it might be said, "Go big or go home!" Greatness doesn't come without a lot of work, a lot of blood, sweat, and tears and usually lots of years of practice. The average "overnight success" has probably been studying and working their craft for years before being recognized for their hard work.

Here's the stunning truth about what it takes to achieve mastery in any field from a great book by Malcolm Gladwell called *Outliers*:

> Researchers have settled on what they believe is the magic number for true expertise: ten thousand hours. "The emerging picture from such studies is that ten thousand hours of practice is required to achieve the level of mastery associated with being a world-class expert in anything," writes the neurologist Daniel Levitin. "In study after study, of composers,

basketball players, fiction writers, ice skaters, concert pianists, chess players, master criminals, and what have you, this number comes up again and again. But no one has yet found a case in which true world-class expertise was accomplished in less time. It seems that it takes the brain this long to assimilate all that it needs to know to achieve true mastery."[1]

Ten thousand hours translates into about ten years of hard work. So, mom and dad, you and junior have your work cut out for you if you want to raise a world changer who is at the top of his field!

The little seed you see when your child is small will either be flourishing or stunted by the time he is twenty-five. I'm well aware each child is different. And success for each one is measured differently. For one, success is measured by the fact they simply finished high school, for another it might be winning an Academy Award for a screenplay, and for another, building an orphanage in a third-world country. Success is doing what God created you to do with passion and fire, in obedience to His will for your life. It won't necessarily fit into the standard American Dream of a mortgage, 2.5 kids, a white picket fence, and the newest iPad! Greatness is deep in each of us in some way. Are you a parent willing to spend the effort and take the time to mine the greatness in your child?

## STEP BY STEP

The dreams your child has at age ten will be refined and refocused at fifteen and fully distilled by the time he is in his twenties. Kids change as they grow. Lots of little boys want to be firemen when they grow up, but only a handful actually *become* firemen. It's the same with little girls. Many dream of being ballerinas. But when they realize how tough it is to make it in the dance world and the sacrifice it will entail to make a career in ballet, most little girls switch to something a lot less physically demanding.

God will use mile markers along the way. What starts out as the dream in a child's heart may not be the ultimate goal for him, but it will help them on their journey. Sometimes the destination changes. But God's economy is never wasteful. He takes the experiences, trials, tragedies, and road bumps in our lives to weave a beautiful tapestry of His purpose if we let Him.

For example, when Francesca was little, she really *did* dream of becoming a ballerina. It was the desire of her heart, and she had the skill and the willingness to put in the work. When she was about twelve, she auditioned for and won a spot at an intense ballet camp in Pennsylvania for the summer. The next year she auditioned for a very exclusive ballet conservatory in Boca Raton, Florida. I really believed at the time God had a professional career in dance as her future. When she didn't get accepted, it was a big surprise to all of us, but at the same time I trusted God had a better plan for her life. In fact, this rejection played a part in helping propel her into music. She had already been taking voice lessons and doing quite a bit of professional theater in and around Orlando. Eventually, because of a physical issue, the option of a future in professional dance fell by the wayside. But as we all know, God may close one door only to open another. Sometimes His *no* leads us into our *yes*!

All along Franny was gaining loads of experience on stage. Every recital, every performance in theater (often doing eight shows a week for six to eight weeks or more), and every performance onstage with the local show choir was preparation for the life on stage she now lives. God knew exactly the training she needed, and while He may have closed some doors, He kept the training going all the while. People so often remark how comfortable she is on stage. It's not a natural gift; it is years of training and years of experience. But it's interesting how God can take a broken dream and make it a doorway into the future! Those years of ballet training prepared her for what she is doing now. She gained confidence, poise, and grace under pressure, and now, going on stage isn't scary; it's home.

Even when things do not work out exactly like you first expected for your child, remember what it says in Romans 8:28: "And we know that all things work together for good to those who love God, to those who are the called according to His purpose." God will sometimes put roadblocks in the way to help change our direction and guide us to His perfect will. At other times, He waits for us to reach a certain level of maturity before He shows His hand and requires us, in His wisdom, to lay down a cherished dream. But His good and perfect plan will always be superior to our best idea of what He has in store for us!

## From Artist to Preacher

Oswald Chambers, the great Scottish author of *My Utmost for His Highest*, originally believed God's call on his life was to be an artist. He studied in Edinburgh for a year but just felt unsettled until he realized, after much wrestling with God, he was called to be a preacher. He struggled for a while until the call became so strong he knew it was God's perfect will for his life. He laid down everything he had worked toward all his life in obedience to God. Imagine if he had continued in art instead of following God's call? We wouldn't have the devotional that's probably impacted more lives than any other in history. He was radically obedient, and God has used his words to influence generations of believers around the world. The lessons he learned and the discipline he mastered to be an artist affected his preaching in a powerful way.

So sometimes what you think you know when your child is small will turn out quite differently when he is grown. God may bring an occasional ninety-degree turn to your plans, but know that everything your child is learning will be brought into the next season. Even when God says no it's all part of His greater plan for your child.

## YOUR BROKEN DREAMS

Be careful you don't allow *your* broken dreams to steal your child's dream for his life. We all have things in our lives that didn't work out. Some obstacles are just too big to overcome, but it doesn't have to be the same story for your child. Teach him to maintain hope and faith and a strong belief in his future and destiny. Some of us missed our opportunities because of sin, lack of belief in ourselves, no motivation, or a host of other reasons. But please don't teach your child there are no happy endings! As the well-known saying goes, "Tough times never last. Tough people do."[2]

The things we've learned through our own disappointments can often be the very tools our children need to plot their own course in life. We can prepare them for the difficulties they are bound to face and equip them with the tools to navigate those disappointments. How we learn to handle disappointment, rejection, and trials is a huge part of our learning process. Difficulties will come, and how our kids handle those difficulties will determine their destiny.

## HAVING A PLAN B

As you see the mighty oak in the tiny acorn, make sure you are equipping your child with the realities of the world he is about to enter. Also, it's good to have a Plan B! In Francesca's case, she was content pursuing the independent artist path. She was well aware how difficult it would be to land a record deal with a major label. Even though it was something I truly believed would happen for her, my husband and I knew enough about the realities of the performing arts world to know how many talented unsigned artists are out there all striving for the same thing. We did as much as we could to keep building her career the old-fashioned way. Then we left it up to the Lord to bring the right connections at the right time. In the meantime, she was faithful to bloom where she was planted.

She played everywhere from big local festivals to small coffee shops to an outdoor shopping area where we helped set up her equipment every Friday night for two years so she could play and sing (in all types of weather) and hopefully sell some CDs. Some Fridays the weather would be great, and she'd gather a big crowd. Other weeks when the weather was cold, she would sing to just a few passersby. But she stuck with it, and there are still people who come up to her today and remark how they remember listening to her sing at Winter Park Village in Florida. She learned perseverance, and because of all the experience she's had singing in every situation you can imagine, there is very little able to surprise her onstage. During this time Franny continued to study and earned her university degree in creative writing, which not only complimented her songwriting but also might have led to other career opportunities if the music road hadn't panned out. Having a Plan B is always a wise idea!

All the experiences your child has while growing up and pursuing his dreams will make him into the person he is destined to become. Every great oak tree has seen its share of storms, droughts, and blizzards. The strong ones get stronger in adversity.

## QUESTIONS TO ASK YOURSELF

1. Am I dreaming too small for my child? How can I dream bigger?

2. Has the destination changed for my child? What do I need to do to adapt?

3. Am I letting past disappointments get in the way?

4. Am I equipping my child with the realities of the world he wants to enter?

5. Am I setting expectations too high or not high enough?

6. Is God taking my child in a new direction? Has He closed one door and opened another?

## PRAYER

*Heavenly Father, I thank You for giving me a big dream for my child. I need Your direction and great discernment in order to help bring this dream to pass. Please show me if disappointments in my life are creating an obstacle for my child. Help me to give my little acorn all the water, sunshine, and good soil he needs to grow into the oak tree You have ordained for him to be. Keep the dream always before me so all I do will help him be the man (or woman) of God You have called him to be. Amen.*

# 4

## PURSUING PURITY IN HEART AND MIND

THERE IS A spiritual battle being waged in our culture for our children's hearts and minds. Raising a child today according to godly standards is going to require parents to buck the crowd and go against societal culture in a myriad of ways. The earlier you begin with your children, the better, because the struggle intensifies the older they get. This can be one of the biggest areas of conflict, especially as your child moves into the middle school and high school years. A lot of your decisions will be based on your child's level of maturity, critical thinking ability, and personal commitment to holiness.

> He who loves purity of heart and has grace on his lips, the king will be his friend.
> —PROVERBS 22:11

I love this scripture, and I wrote my daughter's name right by it in my Bible years ago. I knew God was calling her to something big, and purity of heart, mind, and emotions would be a critical factor in her future. My husband and I knew we needed to be very proactive and discerning with the media and the cultural activities we exposed her to. There are so many ungodly images and temptations coming against our children daily through music, movies, video games, DVDs, social networks, books, and so much more with only one goal: to steal, kill, and destroy your child's destiny, calling, and future. It's a real battle, and as parents, we need to be vigilant at all times and be mindful that purity is of great value to God. Remember, the devil prowls around like a roaring lion seeking whom he will devour!

## What's Your Standard?

When Franny was nine or ten, she had a friend in her ballet class who was allowed to watch pretty much anything she wanted on TV. She was allowed to go to the mall and movies with her friends with no adult chaperones, listen to any kind of music she wanted, and wear pretty much whatever type of clothing she liked. I remember Franny telling me her friend was watching this great new show called *Friends*, and she asked if she could watch it too. "Well," I thought, "let's give it a shot and see what it's like." In the first five minutes I knew this was not going to be a TV show we would be watching in our house! The casual attitudes toward sex, innuendos, and jokes in the first five minutes were enough for me to decide *Friends* was not appropriate in any way for a ten-year-old. We quickly agreed to shut it off.

Kids will be adults far longer than they will be children. What's the rush to expose them to all the junk, sin, and heartache in the world? I'm well aware we can't protect them forever, but I'm a firm believer in letting a child grow up innocent of the ugly side of life until the time comes when she is ready to handle it. I guess my philosophy is to expose her to the world on a need-to-know basis.

## A PARENT'S ROLE

Christian parents have a huge responsibility to set a godly standard in their home and remain consistent. What kind of example do you set when you restrict what your child watches from day to day, yet you and your spouse go out on a Friday night to an R-rated movie, listen to profanity-laced music, or play a violent video game? We made the decision when our daughter was young that we would not have HBO or Showtime in our home, we would not attend R-rated movies, and we would be vigilant about the TV shows we watched and allowed her to watch. Remember, we grew up in the sixties and seventies when "drugs, sex, and rock and roll" were woven into every aspect of society. Because we were saved later in life and we both knew the pitfalls and danger zones prevalent in the world, we were more vigilant than most parents we knew with what we would allow in our home.

When we did watch television, we typically watched as a family and talked about what we saw. We tried to set a wholesome atmosphere where purity was respected, expected, and treasured. Psalm 101:2–3 says it perfectly: "I will walk within my house with a perfect heart. I will set nothing wicked [worthless] before my eyes." Television can be educational and uplifting occasionally, but typically, it can be a huge time waster or an all too convenient babysitter and is, for the most part, a "worthless" thing.

We did not allow a television set or a computer in our daughter's bedroom until she was in college. We were also quite open about monitoring all her computer activity. Franny was living at home before the days of Facebook, Twitter, texting, and most of the current social media, so it was a lot easier to keep up with her. Because we discussed this subject openly, the value of purity was something *she* was passionate about from a young age. This wasn't a particularly difficult area for us as parents, but for many families, it is wise to set parental controls and filtering on the computer and TV. If your children know they are accountable for what they are looking at online and know you will be reviewing it and will be reading their text messages and looking at their Facebook, they will pay a lot more attention to what they are saying and whom they are saying it to. Cyberspace is extremely dangerous and full of pitfalls and predators. As parents we must know what is going on in our children's lives and do all that we can to protect them from every kind of harm. Know what your children are doing online. And let them know you know.

## THREE TYPES OF PARENTS

George Barna, the noted researcher and author, observes in his book *Revolutionary Parenting* there are three approaches to parenting dominant in the United States today:

> One unavoidable influence on parenting behavior is that of societal norms, traditions, and expectations. Because we live within the context of these forces, they have a powerful impact on what we perceive effective parenting to be. Many of these cultural factors are low profile or practically invisible; we practice them simply because we see or experience these elements so frequently in the media or in our daily excursions. Adopting the parenting habits and patterns driven by cultural forces might be described as parenting by default.
>
> The second set of influences that shapes our parenting choices and behaviors is that derived from personal experience and outcomes. Doing

what comes naturally or what we've learned from past endeavors, we raise children in relation to the insights gleaned in the trenches. This trial-and-error process might be considered experimental parenting.

The third approach available to parents, which creates the greatest emotional tension in the parenting marketplace of ideas and practices, comes from the application of biblical commands, principles, and narratives. In this parenting model, God's Word provides the perspective and the marching orders on how to raise a young person. The goal of such child rearing is to raise children who make their faith in God, and relationship with Him, their highest priority in life, and proceed to live as intentional and devoted servants of God. The role of parents is to guide the child to understand the principles and outcomes that honor God and advance His purposes. Success in this venture is measured by transformed lives. I have labeled this one revolutionary parenting.[1]

Revolutionary parenting is clearly the most demanding of the three, but the one that in my opinion bears the most fruit. As you read through these three approaches to parenting, which approach best describes you? If it's parenting by default or trial-and-error parenting, ask God for the help you need to get your family on the right path. Make parenting a "life priority" in your family.

A scripture that we try to live by (one of many) is Philippians 4:8: "Finally, brethren, whatever things are true, whatever things are noble, whatever things are just, whatever things are pure, whatever things are lovely, whatever things are of good report, if there is any virtue and if there is anything praiseworthy—meditate on these things."

I really don't think you can be too careful with a child's media exposure. Even PG-13 movies allow a certain number of profanities and limited nudity in addition to suggestive sexual situations. What about violent video games and profanity-laced music? Television, for the most part, is filled with sexual images, unwholesome family situations, and violence.

Here are some scary statistics on the influence of media on teens.

How much time do teens spend engaged in media?

- Children spend an average of five hours and twenty-three minutes using media every day—watching TV, listening to music, watching videos, using a computer, playing video games.[2]

- Sixty-five percent have a TV in their bedroom.[3]

How much sex is on TV?

- Sexual content appears in two-thirds of all TV programs.[4]

- Programs with sexual content show more than four sex-related scenes an hour.[5]

- Fourteen percent of programs portray sexual intercourse.[6]

- Exposure to high levels of sexual content on television has been shown to be associated with an increased risk of initiating sexual activity, as well as a greater likelihood of involvement in teen pregnancy.[7]

What's the result?
A study conducted in 2006 found that adolescents who were

more exposed to sexuality in the media were also more likely to engage in sexual activity themselves.[8]

What about music?

> Teens who listen to music with sexually explicit and degrading lyrics are more than twice as likely to be having sex. Degrading lyrics were defined as those where sex was described as a physical rather than loving act, and where there was a power differential.
>
> Lyrics describing degrading sex tend to portray sex as expected, direct and uncomplicated. Such descriptions may offer scripts that adolescents feel compelled to play out, whether they are cast in the role of either the female or the male partner.[9]

These frightening statistics should cause all of us to wake up and monitor what we allow into our homes in the way of media. The Bible tells us to "keep your heart with all diligence, for out of it spring the issues of life" (Prov. 4:23). Conduct a family meeting and come up with a list of acceptable TV programs you can watch as a family. List alternative activities you could do together instead of watching TV. How about a family game night? We love to play Scrabble, Backgammon, Life, and Monopoly, and there are dozens of fun games available. What about building something together or teaching your children to sew, cook, or draw? Go outside and learn the constellations. Read together as a family. Volunteer together in your community. You are limited only by your imaginations!

We have to be vigilant and set firm boundaries. Parents need to parent, and we must set absolute standards. As Joshua said, "As for me and my house, we will serve the LORD" (Josh. 24:15). We are parents first, friends later. Unfortunately, many parents compromise in these areas. Here's one depressing way Christian parents compromise every Christmas.

The Barna Group describes it this way in the article dated November 19, 2007: "Christian Parents Are Not Comfortable With Media but Buy Them for Their Kids Anyway."

> Billions of dollars will be spent this Christmas season on gifts for children. A new national study by The Barna Group among Christian parents shows that even though most Christian parents are not always comfortable with the content of the media-related products, they purchase some of those items as presents for their children. The born-again Christian population of the U.S. is likely to spend more than $1 billion on media products such as CDs, DVDs, video games and magazines for children under the age of 18 despite parental misgivings about the moral content or developmental affects of those resources....
>
> "Millions of Christian parents want to appear to be relevant in their children's eyes, and to provide gifts that fit within the mainstream of postmodern society," Barna noted. "The problem is that many of the entertainment products that meet those criteria conflict with the moral precepts of the Christian faith. Parents have to make a choice as to what is more important: pleasing their kids' taste and sensibilities, or satisfying God's standards as defined in the Bible. When the decision made is to keep their children happy, the Christian parent is often left with a pit in their stomach.
>
> "The process of selecting appropriate Christmas presents for children is a microcosm of the spiritual

tension millions of Christian adults wrestle with," the California-based researcher explained. "Many Christian parents are striving to serve two conflicting masters: society and God. They refuse to believe that they cannot satisfy both. Sadly, this Christmas season will produce enormous stress for numerous Christian parents who don't want to disappoint either God or their children, but whose ultimate choices will disappoint both God and themselves, while providing gifts that are not in the best interests of their children. For Christians, the Christmas season should be a time of celebration and appreciation of the life of Jesus Christ. Instead, that joy is being minimized by the pressure and confusion introduced by our focus on material consumption and fulfillment."[10]

How sad. Is it really more important to keep the children happy and thinking you are cool and relevant rather than following biblical standards? Below are more scary statistics that are tough to read but sobering. I include them here because knowledge is power.

- A 2008 study by the Centers for Disease Control and Prevention (CDC) found that one in four teen girls, or an estimated three million girls, has an STD.[11]

- The National Center for Health Statistics has reported that half of all fifteen- to nineteen-year-olds have had oral sex, with the percentage rising to 70 percent by the time they turn nineteen, and equal numbers of boys and girls participating.[12]

- Between the third and tenth grades more than 90 percent of children will be exposed to pornography.[13]

- More than one-fifth of teens have sent sexually suggestive text messages or nude photographs of themselves online.[14]

- In 2009, 46 percent of high school students had ever had sexual intercourse, and 14 percent of high school students had had four or more sex partners during their life. [15] In 2006, an estimated 5,259 young people aged thirteen to twenty-four in the thirty-three states reporting to CDC were diagnosed with HIV/AIDS, representing about 14 percent of the persons diagnosed that year. [16]

- Researchers at Boston College have found that teens who frequently did "things like eating dinner together as a family or engaging in fun activities or religious activities together" were less likely to have sex, had fewer sexual partners, and had less unprotected sex.[17]

Does this wake you up? It did me! To fight our highly sexualized culture, it's imperative we take a radical stand and make a decision to fight the cultural norms with everything we have. My friend Sally, who has done an amazing job raising two children who are faithfully serving the Lord, says it this way:

"Choices and consequences." Our kids heard me say that a million times. We make hundreds of free-will choices a day, from what to wear, whom we hang out with, what to eat, what to say, whom to serve, and the list goes on. But we are not free to choose the consequences of those choices. If we choose to only eat junk food, the consequence is out of our hands. We'll have weight- or health-related problems. If we choose to drink and drive, the consequence is we will likely get pulled over or in an accident. Our kids were cautioned to choose wisely and weigh the consequences of their choice. Once they did that, the wise choice would become evident.

Another good friend Karen, who raised two boys and a girl, tells this story about her son:

> At the high school my son went to, a lot of the boys he knew were having sex with their girlfriends (no surprise there). We would talk to him about what God expected of him. We gave him a book by Josh McDowell to read concerning sexual purity. There was a suggestion line in the book that read, "Anytime I want to I can become like you, but you can never become like me." He said he would say this to his peers when being teased about not having sex. He still was always a popular kid at school even though he would go against the flow. His friends really respected his choice to follow Christ.

## My Thoughts on Homeschooling

My husband and I made a decision when our daughter was young we weren't going to go along with the culture just because it was cool. And that's a big reason why we homeschooled Franny for most of her school years. It was just too important to us she not be influenced unduly by the culture and peer pressure. Not to mention the drug use, rampant sexual experimentation, and violence in many schools.

I realize it's not practical or even possible for every family to homeschool, but if it is possible, I highly recommend looking into it. You remove an awful lot of influences from your children's lives and enable them to grow and learn in a safe, innocent, and parent-directed atmosphere when you homeschool. I love this scripture in Deuteronomy:

> And these words which I command you today shall be in your heart. You shall teach them diligently to your children, and shall talk of them when you sit in your house, when you walk by the way, when you lie down, and when you rise up. You shall bind them as a sign on your hand, and they shall be as frontlets between your eyes. You shall write them on the doorposts of your house and on your gates.
>
> —DEUTERONOMY 6:6–9

This scripture assumes a parent is able to be with their children every day, day in and day out. It speaks of being able to continually have conversations about the things of God in the everyday of daily life. I realize with children attending school five days a week for the better part of forty weeks each year, it will take a serious and dedicated commitment to be part of their day-to-day activities. Too many families hand over too much responsibility to the school or the church to instill basic values. For us, homeschooling was not only a natural choice, since we both worked from home, but it also actually provided the environment for my husband and me to be an integral part of our daughter's most formative years and gave her the opportunity to be involved in professional theater when she was still in middle school.

For the record, I recognize homeschooling may not be the choice or even within the realm of possibility of every family. Two-income families aren't in a position to homeschool for obvious reasons. But for us, it was a natural choice, and one that worked well for Franny, freeing her up to become more deeply involved in dance, theater, and music. We homeschooled her from kindergarten through third grade. She went to private Christian school from fourth through seventh grade and was homeschooled again from eighth grade until graduation.

A press release from the Home School Legal Defense Association (HSLDA) gives some great support to the value of homeschooling. HSLDA released the following study entitled the Progress Report 2009:

> "Homeschool Academic Achievement and Demographics," conducted by Dr. Brian Ray of the National Home Education Research Institute, which surveyed 11,739 homeschooled students for the 2007–08 academic school year. The results were consistent with previous studies on homeschool academic achievement and showed that homeschoolers, on average, scored 37 percentile points above public school students on standardized achievement tests.
>
> "These results validate the dedication of hundreds of thousands of home school parents who are giving their children the best education possible," said Michael Smith, president of HSLDA.
>
> The Progress Report drew homeschoolers from 15 independent testing services and is the most comprehensive study of home school academic achievement ever completed.
>
> While the academic results are impressive, the

study also showed that the achievement gaps common to public schools were not found in the home school community.

Homeschooled boys (87th percentile) and girls (88th percentile) scored equally well; the income level of parents did not appreciably affect the results (household income under $35,000: 85th percentile—household income over $70,000: 89th percentile); and while parent education level did have some impact, even children whose parents did not have college degrees scored in the 83rd percentile, which is well above the national average for public school students. Homeschooled children whose parents both had college degrees scored in the 90th percentile.

"Because of the one-on-one instruction homeschoolers receive, we are prepared academically to be productive and contributing members of today's society," said Smith.

The average public school spends nearly $10,000 per child per year whereas the Progress Report shows that the average home school parent spends about $500 per child per year.

"Homeschooling is a rapidly growing, thriving education movement that is challenging the conventional wisdom about the best way to raise and educate the next generation," said Smith.

There are an estimated 2 million homeschooled children in the U.S. today, which is about 4 percent of the school-aged population, and homeschooling is growing at around 7% per year.[18]

The common argument that says homeschooled kids are somehow handicapped in the area of socialization simply doesn't hold water. Like many areas where homeschooling has taken firm root, Orlando has a variety of excellent homeschool support organizations with programs that not only support important educative goals but also incorporate organized team sports, band and music programs, science labs, and lots more. Most homeschooled kids I've spent time with are among the most socially adept young people I know, and they're at ease in a variety of social situations. Perhaps it's because homeschooled kids spend a good amount of time among adults in the real world and with a parent or two who model real-life, everyday adult interaction. An added benefit in Franny's homeschooling experience was she not only excelled in her studies with straight As but also finished high school a full year early.

I've known Barbara and her husband, Chris, for many years. She's a homeschooling mom and music teacher, and he has the unique job of putting in audio and video systems in theme parks around the world. She shares her experience homeschooling her three children:

> In order to balance our lives with Chris working and traveling and me teaching music every afternoon and ministering often, we've made a very important decision to deliberately spend time with our children— Nathan (eighteen), Sam (fifteen), and Emily (ten). The most important decision we've made is to homeschool our children. Homeschooling allows us to make the most of the time my husband is home. We also get to visit the attractions my husband works on while we are schooling. We live in the sunny state of Florida. Chris works on many of the local theme parks such as Disney, Universal Studios, and the Kennedy Space Center. He also goes across the United States, so our children have visited the Smithsonian museums,

Hard Rock Park, the Georgia Museum, the Coca-Cola museum, and New York City over the years.

When we are not traveling, we enjoy learning together at home and taking some classes with friends. To many people, homeschooling seems to be a daunting task. How could you possibly have several children at home, learning different topics at different grade levels? Personally, I throw out the "public school" way of doing things. We learn topics at the same time. If my boys are learning biology, I also teach biology to my younger daughter. I have always had my boys take the same math at the same time. When we pick subjects for history, science, or even literature and grammar, we often do these things together, which saves me time and energy—one plan for all my children. I expect more knowledge and writing out of my older children, but, at their ages, they can learn together.

There is a saying that says, "It takes a village to raise a child." I've found it very helpful to do certain classes with other families. It's good for my boys to do classes with students their own age. Sometimes, it's good to have your child learn from another teacher or in a group setting because they will give a better answer to someone else. I guess you'd call that positive peer pressure. Over the years, I've founded and organized homeschool class co-ops so parents can share the load of teaching their kids. The most recent co-op I organized ended up having twenty-five families, with sixty students K–12. So many gifted moms were able to help teach in a fun, encouraging environment. Working together also allowed my children and other students to delve into their gifts and talents.

My children are very different from one another. Nathan is gifted in computers, graphics, Web design, film, and guitar. Sam is a versatile musician, playing electric and acoustic guitar, keyboards, and most often drums. He also is very photogenic and enjoys acting. Emily loves to sing, dance, and perform. We've found a variety of ways to help our children grow in their gifts. Our homeschool classes provide a place for Web design and video classes, actor/improvisation class with an amazing comedian, and worship team class to develop vocal and instrument skills. Emily takes dance class. All my children sing and play for worship teams at many churches. Nathan, who interned for a Web design firm, now designs graphics and websites for many family friends. Every year we go to the Gideon Film Festival (Christian filmmakers, writers, actors, and musicians) for film and acting school. My children and I work as background extras in several films shooting in the Orlando area. All of this allows us to have life, and have it to the full, and pursue God's dream for each one of us. (See John 10:10.)

## BE THE "COOL" PARENTS

I'm the kind of mom who always loved having my daughter's friends over, and they loved to come to our house. I believed it was important to stay in touch with whom she was spending time with, and I couldn't think of a better way than to be the host house for any gathering. When the youth group needed a place for Sunday night meetings, I eagerly volunteered our home. My couch didn't hold up so well against the antics of teenage boys, and it still bears the scars, but I was able to get to know the kids in my daughter's life!

I loved being the "cool" mom with the "cool" house. Franny's friends would invite me into their Clue games and conversations. I always had yummy food on hand for the kids and loved to have them stay for dinner whenever possible, and I was willing to do whatever it took to help them all have a great time. There are a few girls from those days who will still e-mail me from time to time and just want to know if they can come over for dinner and hang out—with me! Franny doesn't live here anymore but they want to see me...and Mike too! It blesses me incredibly to know the impact I had years ago still bears fruit today. And they invite me to their weddings and showers!

I was blessed when Franny was growing up and I didn't have to work outside the home. Because I didn't, I was available to volunteer to chaperone for every field trip, I could drive her to every ballet class and every rehearsal and voice lesson. I put tons of miles on my car, but I also gained great insight into adolescence and the teenage and young adult years by being welcoming and available to my daughter and her friends. Be the house everyone wants to come to, and you will be amazed the impact you'll have and the lasting relationships you'll develop. Plus, when all the kids are over at your house, you know exactly where they are!

Mike and I made it a point to meet the parents of Franny's friends. We wanted to know the families and discern if going to their house was going to be an option for her. It's important to know whom your kids are spending time with and if they hold the same values as you do. The last thing you want to do is to take such care in your own home and then send them over to a friend's house where they think nothing of watching R-rated movies and love playing violent video games. Know the character of the people you are letting your children spend time with.

My friend Sally agrees.

Never did my kids go to anyone's home before I knew all the details and felt comfortable with them. I would not rely on hearsay but would always contact (by phone in those days!) the parent to verify the details. Our kids knew it wasn't because we didn't trust them but because we cared.

## ABSTINENCE AND PURITY RINGS

Abstinence and purity were a big focus in our house, and when Franny turned thirteen, her dad took her on her first date. She put on a brand-new, pretty flowered dress and heels, and dad put on a suit and took her to a fancy restaurant for dinner. They talked and chatted about everything under the sun and enjoyed a lovely meal together. Then he got serious. A few weeks before, he and I had ordered a beautiful 14 karat gold ring for her that looked like a small gift-wrapped heart. He spoke to her about the importance of keeping herself pure until marriage and prayed a prayer of blessing over her. He had written up a commitment for her to sign, which was her promise to him to remain pure until she got married. Then he asked her to sign the agreement, which she willingly did. Afterward he presented her with her beautiful ring. He gently put it on her ring finger explaining how on the day she got married she could present her ring to her husband as a symbol of her love and the commitment she made to wait for him. Until that day, her heart would remain securely gift-wrapped and waiting for her husband.

She wore that ring for eleven years. For her husband-to-be, she did something very special and beautiful with the ring. Before her wedding Franny took her gold gift-wrapped heart to the jeweler and had him melt it down and actually put it inside her husband's wedding ring as a band of gold that's an integral part of his ring. It cannot be separated, and you can see it if you look at the inside of his ring. The symbol of her commitment to him is forever melded together in his ring, a constant reminder how she was faithful to wait for him. Of course, he was incredibly touched by what she had done.

Children need and want boundaries and guidance in this crazy world we live in. They need our help making sense of all the mixed signals bombarding them every day. Determine what the standards are going to be in your household, be consistent, and spend as much time as you can with your kids. If you have more than one, take time each day to talk to them, listen to them, and pray with them. Be as involved in their lives as time permits, and let them know how much you value them. Get to know their friends and their parents. Make a commitment to purity a standard in your household, and be bold in standing up to a culture that does all it can to destroy it.

## QUESTIONS TO ASK YOURSELF

1. What's the biggest cultural battle facing my family?

2. How can I be more proactive in promoting purity in my child?

3. What negative influence has the media had on my child, and what changes can we make as a family to combat it?

4. Are my spouse and I consistently setting a godly standard in our home when it comes to the media and culture?

5. Are we vigilant about the media influences we allow in, and are we using parental controls on TVs and computers?

6. Which of the three parenting types defines me and my spouse?

7. How much TV are my children watching each week? What are some alternative activities we can do as a family?

8. Do my children's friends love to spend time at my house? Am I the "cool home"? If not, why not?

9. Do I know the parents of my children's friends?

10. Have I talked to my teens about abstinence, purity, and saving sex until marriage?

# PRAYER

*Lord, we come before You with humility. Your Word says if we lack wisdom to ask, and You will give it to us liberally. So we ask for Your wisdom to know, Lord, what is acceptable in Your sight. Help us to set godly boundaries in our homes to protect our children from the filth of the world. Continue to help us promote purity and its value to our children. Give us the boldness and the confidence to stand against the cultural norms and to protect our children from influences that only seek to harm them and steal their futures. Give us eyes to see and ears to hear, and let us lovingly set a standard of purity in our household. Let this scripture become our standard: "Whatever things are true, whatever things are noble, whatever things are just, whatever things are pure, whatever things are lovely, whatever things are of good report, if there is any virtue and if there is anything praiseworthy—meditate on these things" (Phil. 4:8).*

# 5

# TOOLS OF THE TRADE

I THINK THE BEST way to illustrate the principles of this chapter is through sharing stories of what my husband and I did to equip our daughter by providing the best tools and experiences we could afford. This chapter will be a little heavier on the stories, but I think sometimes it's easier for someone to understand if you show rather than tell them. So here goes!

When Franny was sixteen, she wanted to learn to play the guitar. Knowing her to be diligent in whatever she was interested in, Mike and I took her to Guitar Center and helped her pick out a decent but not expensive Yamaha. It cost around three hundred dollars, and we considered it a good investment in her future. She began to take lessons, and before long she was doing some serious practicing and writing for hours in her bedroom.

Not too long after that, a musical mentor we thought highly of was holding a three-day conference for independent musicians in Las Vegas. By this time Franny seriously aspired to be a singer-songwriter. We knew there was a lot we needed to learn to be able to guide her properly through the world of independent music. We registered for the conference and booked our flights and hotel, and off we went.

All three of us experienced an eye-opening time of learning, growing, and networking. Franny was the youngest performer at the conference and made a paradigm-shifting discovery while there. The conference leader asked anyone who desired to sign up to perform for their peers during certain sessions, and he allowed the other attendees to critique their performances. She wanted so badly to do it but was scared to pieces because she had never played guitar for anyone other than mom and dad and was petrified she would by slammed by the other more seasoned musicians.

## STEPPING OUT OF HER COMFORT ZONE

We had befriended a young couple at the conference, and the husband worked with Franny on her song and convinced her she was ready to perform. With trembling hands and wobbly knees she got up in front of one hundred other aspiring musicians—all with years more experience—and she sang and played her heart out. When she was done, everyone was blown away by her age and ability. But more importantly, she came away grateful she mustered the courage to step out of her comfort zone and perform. She was humbled by the affirmation of her peers. She was more convinced than ever she was on the right path and knew then and there music was her destiny.

I'm so grateful we took the time and spent the money for the three of us to share such an important growing experience together. She learned a vital lesson during the conference, and she has never forgotten it. She learned if you're afraid, that's OK. Do it afraid! She proved something to herself, and she boldly stepped out of her comfort zone, which is worth any amount of money in my book!

By the time her eighteenth birthday rolled around, Mike and I wanted to do something really special for her. By now, music and songwriting had become her full-blown passion. We strongly sensed the Lord taking her in this direction, so we wanted to mark the occasion and also let her know we were as seriously committed to her dreams as she was. What did it mean to us? It meant purchasing a top-of-the-line acoustic guitar. At that time we were pretty strapped financially, but I had a good friend in the fragrance business who gave me lots of part-time work so I could save up the money to buy Franny a top-of-the-line guitar.

When her birthday arrived, we were able to take her back to Guitar Center to buy her a beautiful three-thousand-dollar Taylor acoustic guitar she still plays today. If you've seen her in concert, you've seen her play the guitar we gave her on her eighteenth birthday. It serves as a perfect illustration for what this chapter is all about—providing the absolute best tools you can possibly afford to fuel your child's dreams.

I worked lots of hours to save up enough money to buy her the guitar. Lots of Saturdays and afternoons at the mall selling perfume and standing on my feet all day, but you know what? It's totally worth it. Before she ever had a record deal, she had a professional level guitar, and I know it helped equip her for success.

Another way to value your child's gifts and callings is to do what my friend Corey and her husband did for their daughter. Corey says:

> Randy and I have a family with a legacy of min-
> istry we have felt Rachel will walk in. We have
> been unwavering in our belief that God has some-
> thing extraordinary for her in other countries. When
> she has expressed a desire to travel to a particular
> one, we have done everything possible to make it
> happen. And while it has not yet come to fruition,

we have even arranged for her to live overseas if she chooses to do so. Rachel's first trip out of the country without us was the first time she bumped into her destiny. Each time she has traveled since then, in every country she has visited, she has continued to have a sense of being home. Her heart has become attached to the people, and she has seen her future entwined with theirs.

Now that's putting your money where your mouth is!

Mike and I have always valued our daughter's interests. When she studied ballet and really believed she would grow up to have a professional career in dance, we provided the best pointe shoes, leotards, and lessons we could afford. We sent her to a wonderful ballet camp in Philadelphia one summer and made sure she had costumes for all her recitals. If you currently have a daughter in ballet, you know those costumes are expensive! We constantly let her know we respected what she valued.

## EVERYTHING OLD IS NEW AGAIN

When Franny was eleven years old, she was part of a local show choir sponsored by the Orlando Civic Theater called Civic Kids. They performed at all kinds of functions for the city of Orlando, and she got a lot of great performing experience with them. Many of the kids were involved in doing local commercials, television, and theater. One day she came home from rehearsal to tell me the area dinner theater company was planning to produce a revival of *The Sound of Music*. She asked if we could audition.

Wow, she brought me back to my past in a hurry! Early in my career I had played Liesl in a dinner theater production of *The Sound of Music*, and I had a great love for the show. Franny really wanted to audition, but she was a little scared to do it alone, so she asked me to audition too. I knew I was too old at this point to play Liesl, or even Maria for that matter, but maybe I could play the mean Baroness. Well, off we went to the auditions, and wouldn't you know, we both got cast—she as Marta (one of the children) and me as the mean Baroness. You should have seen my wig!

Anyway, all that to say, sometimes you have to go *way* out of your way to make your child's dream come to pass. I wasn't looking to get back into theater, but I certainly didn't want her in the theater world by herself, since I knew well the pitfalls and dangers lurking there. But I also know there is a wonderful sense of community and family that exists in the theater world. Not to mention the onstage experience she would gain. And on top of it all, we both got paid!

We did a wonderful production of *I Remember Mama* the next year. I was cast as "Mama" and Franny was one of the four children in the show. A few years later, we were cast together again in a production of *Ben-Hur: The Musical*, which was locally produced in Orlando but had a Broadway caliber cast and a nine-million-dollar budget. *Ben-Hur* provided our family the unique experience of all three of us taking our bows at the same curtain call—with Franny and me on stage and Mike on the conductor's podium before a twenty-eight-piece pit orchestra. Perhaps we will be given the opportunity to do that again one day. I hope so.

To Franny, being on stage is home. She gained so much performing experience with those wonderful opportunities to sing and dance as a youngster. Being in front of a live audience so frequently during her early years fueled her passion for theater and live performance and is a primary reason she is so focused, secure, and comfortable on stage today. These experiences also contributed to putting a dent in the ten thousand hours referenced in Malcolm Gladwell's *Outliers*. It also drew us closer together as a family because we all shared the same passion.

It didn't surprise us when it came time for Franny to vote for where she'd like to go on vacation. She always asked to go to New York City to eat at John's Pizza on Bleecker Street (the *best* pizza) and go see Broadway shows—this in spite of being blessed to live in Orlando, where so many families from all over the world choose to vacation.

What about your children? What are their passions? Has God begun to show you His purpose for their lives as you prayed for them? Are you doing all you can to fuel their dreams? If sports is their passion, are you as involved as you can possibly be in their sport? Participating with them is time well invested, even if it's just to carpool to practices or chaperone away games or competitions. Being able to actually coach your child's sport is a tremendous way to be involved, especially for dads.

Whatever their passion, there is certainly some way for you to share it with them. To the best of your ability, do whatever you can to provide the tools and instruction to help your children excel. At one point during her adolescent years, Franny was busily involved in taking dance classes, acting classes, commercial classes, and voice lessons all at the same time. The financial and time commitment accompanying those lessons was our investment in her future. We purposed to do whatever we possibly could to give wings to her dreams.

## THE DREAM DRAWS CLOSER

The summer after she turned eighteen, we went to Estes Park, Colorado. Until recently the Gospel Music Association hosted an annual weeklong conference in beautiful Estes Park called Music in the Rockies for aspiring Christian musicians. The conference offered wonderful seminars and classes, a variety of songwriting and singing categories to compete in as well as concerts every evening with the top headlining artists in Christian music. Registration began in February for the August conference, and as I read more about it on their website, the stronger sense I had from the Lord this was something we needed to do as a family. I talked with Mike and Franny, and after praying about it, we all agreed it was something we were supposed to attend. By this time Franny had finished writing and recording her first full-length independent record.

When August rolled around, we headed off to the mountains of Colorado, excited about our time away as a family and for what we would learn during the weeklong retreat. During the registration process, Franny had entered both the songwriting competition and the singing competition. We arrived on a Sunday, and in the evening everyone gathered in the big auditorium for the announcement of whose songs had been chosen to be judged in the competition rounds. If your song was chosen, it was played before a panel of industry professionals and critiqued by them. And if it survived the first-round critique, it would then move to the next round. There were hundreds of singer-songwriters, many who attended year after year hoping for a break. Holding our breath, we were excited to hear the name Francesca Battistelli announced in the worship song category. So many talented artists came back every year whose songs were never chosen, and here she was her first year out having one of her songs chosen to advance. So far, with arrival day behind us, we were all pretty excited!

The next day was her first day to sing in front of a music industry panel of agents, producers, label execs, and professional songwriters. Each day, as the judges listened to the competitors, they would choose a handful of artists to perform in a special nighttime cabaret showcase. It was an opportunity for all the industry professionals to attend and hear the new up-and-coming talent. The first day of competition Franny was chosen for that night's showcase! Her performance at the cabaret was heard by a man who would open some important doors for her in Nashville in the years to come. He took an interest in Franny and gave her a hand up and helped her to network in Nashville. He even invited her to a record label retreat in Washington State the following year. If we hadn't obeyed the leading of the Lord back in February and registered for the conference, this "divine appointment" might never have occurred.

All in all, the Estes Park week was a fantastic experience for her. Though she didn't win in her categories, Franny made friends and priceless contacts and gained vital experience that contributed to her future success. On a side note, this is the same year *American Idol* winner Jordin Sparks and *American Idol* alumni Chris Sligh and Phil Stacey competed, although a few years before any of them appeared on *American Idol*.

Our goal as parents was to find fertile ground for her gifts to grow. As we had been faithful to mine the gifts in her, God now provided the experiences and teachers to cut and polish the stone of her calling and begin making it into a beautiful gem. We were always ready to make a financial investment into her future in practical ways, even when times were tough and dollars were scarce. Because of the connections we made in Colorado, Franny was invited to come to Nashville the following February to showcase at another Gospel Music Association event. During her time in Nashville, she was given the unique opportunity of writing with two professional songwriters. A few years later, one of them ended up cowriting several songs on her first album!

## WHAT YOU CAN DO

I realize most of you are not raising a child to go into the music business. But what are some things you can do as a parent to help your child fulfill his dreams and destiny? Look for opportunities within your community in your child's area of interest where he might become involved. Is there somewhere to intern over the summer that might provide valuable experience and contacts for his future? Are there camps, conferences, or conventions in his field of interest? What about books, magazine subscriptions, or online resources? You never know the one piece of the puzzle or the one person he might meet or work with who can provide the bridge to his future success.

One last thing: as parents, we owe it to our children to learn as much as we can about their chosen field. Our professional background gave us a lot of knowledge about the business of theater but not much about the contemporary music industry. I think my husband bought every book written at the time about the music industry, record labels, record deals, artist management, touring, and songwriting—and he read every one of them! I'm so grateful he did, because when the time came for Franny to sign her record deal, he was well educated and had an authentic understanding of recording and publishing contracts and the music business in general. As a result, he was able to help Franny navigate her way through the entire complex process. When it was time to assemble a team of experienced professionals around her, we were delighted how God brought just the right people to come alongside and partner with her. Until then, Mike happily wore multiple hats and served as personal manager, business manager, booking agent, and roadie, and made learning about the music world his priority in order to go to bat for her, negotiate for her, and protect her interests.

We were as involved as parents can be in our daughter's life all during these important years. We looked at it as a great privilege and sacred trust from the Lord to steer her into her career and to know we were doing all we could to mine the greatness in her. While Mike and I are no longer involved in the everyday business of Franny's career, we remain her strongest supporters and proudest cheerleaders.

## QUESTIONS TO THINK ABOUT

1. What tools have you provided to fuel your child's dream?

2. What tools would you like to provide, and what can you do to provide them?

3. How are you valuing your child's interests?

4. How can you better share your child's passion?

5. What are some practical ways you can provide fertile ground for your child's gifts to grow?

6. In what ways can you learn more about your child's chosen field?

7. Are you willing to make a financial investment in your child's future?

## PRAYER

*Lord, as You've helped me to see the gifts residing in my child, please show me practical ways I can make his gifting shine! Give me the financial resources to provide the fuel for my child's dreams. Help me to learn everything I can about the things he is passionate about and to provide the good soil his gifts need in which to grow and develop. Above all, let me be an enthusiastic voice of encouragement to him to help him face any fears and overcome whatever obstacles may come.*

# BE AVAILABLE

W E LIVE IN a busy world, chock-full of distractions, to-do lists, and time-wasters. So many things conspire to steal our time and attention, causing us to waste precious hours we will never get back. Social networking comes to mind as one of those things valuable for sharing news or asking for prayer, but it can become for some of us a huge time-waster. I admit to being active on both Facebook and Twitter, and it's been a great way to stay in touch with friends as well as my daughter's busy schedule. But can you honestly tell me the value of spending countless mindless hours on games such as FarmVille or Mafia Wars?

I can certainly find myself spending *way* too much time on Facebook or Twitter while the important things, the pressing items on my to-do list, remain undone.

What about television? There are so many sitcoms, sporting events, cooking shows, reality programs, and do-it-yourself shows to watch and so little time to see them all. My personal favorite guilty pleasures and time-wasters happen to be watching *Ice Road Truckers* on TV and playing Spider Solitaire, but that's another story!

Other than being available for our spouses and making time

for the Lord each day, when it comes to our kids, spending time with them is priority one. Parents have precious few years to influence their values, help shape their dreams, and model the moral code and work ethic we live by. We shouldn't let anything take precedence over spending time with them. Our priorities must include our children, especially while they still live under our roof, absorbing the most important influence in their young lives—ours! Being available at each stage of their development is just as important as the next.

My friend Patricia, with tongue slightly in cheek and having raised three kids mostly as a single mom, says it like this:

> Love them hard, inspect what you expect, and be clear when you give direction. Kids want discipline, yet they will never say so. They need structure. And when they make a big mistake, tell them you love them and that is why they must take responsibility for their actions. They hate that. If you have more than one child, make special individual time for each. Go to a movie or a game. Have an ice cream date or make a meal together for the rest of the family. When a really tough situation arises and your child has really blown it and made a bad decision, start to cry and blame yourself. Say that you must have failed as a parent and make sure your nose is really runny. The self-guilt angle works every time.

How involved should you be? As involved as you possibly can! The more children you have, the thinner you will be stretched, but making time each week to be available for your children and their activities is critical. Teens especially need time with mom and dad.

In her article "Ten Things Teens Wish Their Parents Knew" author Meghan Vivo says:

### Number 9: Teens care what their parents think.

Peers have a great deal of influence on your teen, but studies show you have more. For example, in a 2004 National Campaign to Prevent Teen Pregnancy study, less than one-third of teens cited friends as having the most impact on their decisions about sex, while nearly half of teens said their parents were the most influential.

According to Project Teen Canada, a decades-long study of 5,500 Canadian teenagers, nine out of 10 teens describe their mothers as having a high level of influence in their lives, and eight in 10 say the same of their fathers. In addition, teens reported fewer arguments and feeling less misunderstood by their parents in 2008 than in previous years.

Adolescents who are strongly connected to their parents perform better in school and are less likely to smoke, abuse drugs and engage in other destructive behaviors. Even if you feel you've lost all influence, keep talking, your teens are listening.

### Number 10: Your teen really loves you.

Your teen may not show it, but they really do love you. As they grow into adults, they pull away so they can establish their own identity. Don't take the distance personally. You are the most important person in your child's life, and staying connected during adolescence means even closer bonds in adulthood.[1]

## WHO HAS THE TIME?

Each week has exactly 168 hours. Assuming work (or school), travel, and sleep occupy 106 of those hours (40, 10, and 56, respectively), we're left with 62 hours. Housework, shopping, meal preparation, and other chores will take up a chunk of the time remaining. Some of us also need to sneak a little "me" time in there just to maintain our sanity and recharge our batteries. Don't forget time alone with your spouse!

Allocating these remaining hours can take some serious balancing, but the good news is we get fifty-two opportunities every year to get it right. And I can't think of anything *more* right than spending as many of these hours as possible being available to our kids. Sometimes it doesn't even have to be "quality" time. Regular, consistent time spent listening, loving, and teaching our kids is more valuable than gold—and will pay dividends for years and perhaps generations to come.

My friend Sally fondly remembers her time spent driving her kids to school:

> The kids went to a private Christian school about thirty minutes from home. I never begrudged that drive. I loved that hour a day of "captivity," particularly on the drive home. This was the time I could just listen to them unload and decompress and also interject ideas and suggestions if necessary. I loved all ten years of that!

As a mom, it was my priority to be as involved in my daughter's life as much as possible without being smothering. There is a phenomenon known as the "helicopter parent," described in Wikipedia as "a colloquial, early twenty-first-century term for a parent who pays extremely close attention to his or her child's or children's experiences and problems, particularly at educational institutions."[2] This type of parent hovers over every aspect of their child's existence to an unhealthy degree—certainly not what I'm suggesting.

As a homeschooling family we enjoyed lots of added togetherness that might not be available if your kids attend school. I think if you asked Franny about it, she would say it was a good thing. I was blessed to be a stay-at-home mom and not have to work outside the house. Mike ran a business and worked from home during those years, so we had lots of opportunities to go on field trips, sometimes as a family. We had lots of hours in the car driving to a myriad of classes, lessons, and rehearsals. The car for most moms is already their home away from home, but we always tried to make it a fun family experience as much as possible. Still today we play some of the same silly word games invented during the many hours in the family minivan.

## What's Most Important?

We decided early on what was important to our daughter would be important to us. Kids deeply care about what their parents think, particularly when it comes to their ideas and the dreams they have for their lives. They really do want to spend time with you, as long as they don't fear being constantly judged, nagged, or criticized, especially about their dreams. We need to be extra careful not to belittle our child's feelings, especially during those delicate preteen and teenage years when they are trying so hard to find their own identity. They need, above all, to feel that you are a safe sounding board, someone who will give them thoughtful advice and someone who will listen twice as much as you speak (after all, in God's perfect economy He gave us two ears and one mouth).

When Franny was in middle school, she attended a Christian

school for a few years. I would pick her up each day after school, and some days I noticed she was really quiet and subdued. I learned not to press her for conversation on those days, but just get her home or to dance class. At some point during the afternoon or evening I knew if I was patient she would open up and download everything she was feeling. I learned to wait for her to signal she was ready to talk. And when she was, I would drop what I was doing to give her my complete attention. I wanted her to know she could trust me to value her feelings and hear her out and she could rely on me to give her good advice and counsel and a loving ear. Because I grew up in a very critical atmosphere, I worked hard to avoid doling out careless criticism. I knew firsthand the damage it does, and I didn't want to purposely inflict it on my child. I was not always successful with this, and Franny would probably be the first to tell you I'm far from perfect, but I tried hard to let my words speak encouragement and life, not death.

If we were confused about a situation or how to handle it, we would go to the Word to see what God had to say about it. I also had developed a circle of friends and trusted advisers who were always a source of godly counsel. Connecting with other like-minded parents who may have already experienced what you're struggling with can be an incredible lifeline.

We took great interest in the things Franny was passionate about, which was music and the arts. Our interest came naturally and was easy for us because it was right in line with what we already loved. What if your child has a burning interest in and is excited about a subject you know nothing about and could care less about? What do you do? Well, you learn about it, do the best you can to understand it, and dig into it with both hands right alongside your child! What a great way to spend time learning something new and demonstrating to your child her importance to you. I'm grateful Franny wasn't drawn to math or science! I don't know how I would have motivated her since I was not proficient in either subject. It wouldn't have been a particularly easy task, but I would have pressed in and done the best I could to be interested in and discover math's mysteries along with her. If she had wanted to be a microbiologist or set her sights on becoming a doctor or lawyer, we would have found opportunities to explore those subjects. We do these things not only to honor and value the call on our child's life and demonstrate respect for what interests her, but also for the lasting memories of special time spent learning something new together.

Think how empowering it is to your child for you to tangibly share her excitement about a subject! At the very least, go to the library or get on the Internet and start learning about whatever it is that's capturing her interest. Find some research on the subject, look for local classes you can take, order a magazine subscription for her and for you. Actions really *do* speak louder than words.

## Goals and Expectations

One of the most treasured gifts we can give to our children is to teach them the value of setting goals. If they don't know their destination, how will they ever know when they get there? Stephen Covey describes goal setting in his book *The Seven Habits of Highly Effective People* in this way:

> An effective goal focuses primarily on results rather than activity. It identifies where you want to be, and, in the process, helps you determine where you are. It gives you important information on how to get there, and it tells you when you have arrived. It unifies your efforts and energy. It gives meaning and purpose to all you do. And it can finally translate itself into daily activities so that you are proactive, you are in charge of your life, you are making happen each day

the things that will enable you to fulfill your personal mission statement.[3]

We've long believed in and practiced goal setting in our family. Statistics abound indicating those who set written goals are drawn like magnets to their inevitable completion. There are so many great resources available on goal setting, but here is a basic outline to get you started if this is new for you.

1. State your goal as a positive statement.

2. Be precise and specific. Use dates, times, and amounts so you can measure your results.

3. Prioritize your goals and revisit them regularly.

4. Write your goals and put them in a place where you can see them.

5. Lay out the steps you need to take to achieve your goals.

6. Set deadlines and attach intermediate time lines to your goals.

7. Consider obstacles to your goals and develop a plan to deal with them.

Here's an example. Say you have a fourteen-year-old who is hoping to go to college. The big goal is "I will go to college in four years." What are the necessary steps to achieve that goal? They might look like this:

1. Take college prep classes during high school.

2. Start saving money now and learn about financial aid and scholarships.

3. Diligently work to complete homework, study, and go to class every day.

4. Become involved in extracurricular and community activities.

5. Apply to colleges with the assistance of school counselors and parents.

6. Finish high school.

Each of these steps can be broken down even further, but you get the point. Two of Franny's goals during her teenage years were to make an album of original songs and sign a record deal with a major label. To achieve these, she set subordinate goals including:

1. Practice guitar and piano for a set time each day.

2. Write a certain amount each week.

3. Go to the gym at least three times a week.

4. Complete all required school work each day.

5. Sing, write, and work on music every day.

A simple acronym I like reminds us goals should be SMART:

- Specific

- Measurable

- Attainable

- Relevant

- Time sensitive

We have always been a goal-setting family, and we've seen the power of it over and over again in multiple areas of our lives—personal, financial, spiritual, and physical. A great exercise to do with the whole family is to write down some family goals and brainstorm to come up with specific, measurable ways the family can work together to achieve them. We always enjoyed sitting down to share our personal and family goals, and we did it often. We would try to start each new year with a fresh review of where we were, which goals had been attained, and how to plot our course for the coming year. January 1 of every year always held great anticipation of what the coming year might bring, and I heartily recommend making something like this a tradition in your home.

## BE THE INVOLVED PARENT

Parents who are involved in their children's lives are much more in touch with the way their dreams and desires for their lives are evolving. One of the best ways to be involved is take time to volunteer at their school. Be the parent who is available to the best of your ability. Check their homework. Read their papers and offer praise and constructive ways to make their work even better. Go on field trips. I made it a point to always be a chaperone mom even on those long (and uncomfortable) bus trips to Washington DC! We share so many great memories from those days, and I am grateful to have had the opportunity to spend time with my daughter and really get to know many of her friends very well. As often as possible I volunteered to drive or carpool, and it gave us precious time together.

## BE THEIR BIGGEST FAN

Now, with an empty nest, I'm especially glad we had those times together. The years will fly by, and your children will move into the life God has prepared for them before you know it, so take every opportunity to spend time with them now. Nothing is more valuable to them than your time and attention. Being with them speaks volumes about their worth in your eyes and builds their self-esteem. So often kids, teens especially, feel badly about themselves. They are constantly comparing themselves to others at school and assessing how they measure up.

We have the great opportunity to be our children's biggest fan! Let them know you delight in them. Remind them daily how wonderful, how special, and how unique they are. Remember, words have tremendous power, and what we say today has significant impact on their tomorrow. Open communication with our kids is key. Be honest about your expectations and values, and listen, listen, *listen* to what they have to say! Disagree when appropriate. Empathize when needed. Redirect stray ideas. But above all be a consistent communication partner with your children. As they open up, your kids will share their struggles and fears, joys and accomplishments, hopes, heartaches, and grief.

## You're Not Them

One more thing I learned on this journey of being Franny's mom? I'm not her. My personality is *very* different. I came to the realization a few years back that I'm a fixer, a problem solver, and solution oriented. Every time she came to me to share something on her heart or a problem she was dealing with, I tried to solve it. It's just the way I'm wired, I guess. But sometimes she didn't want a solution; sometimes she just wanted me to listen and give her a hug and tell her I loved her. Sometimes I simply *couldn't* fix it! And it was OK, because she didn't need it to be fixed. She just needed her mom to listen and empathize.

Our children will grow up and eventually have to figure things out for themselves. Our job is to remember we aren't them, and we can't solve every problem or remove every obstacle. We have to live our own lives, not theirs. I think it particularly applies if you are the parent of an only child. It's easy to become so wrapped up in your child's life that you lose your focus.

## QUESTIONS TO THINK ABOUT

1. What are the biggest time wasters and distractions I'm facing?

2. How involved am I in my child's life? Am I too involved or not enough?

3. If I break down the hours available to me each week, is there more time I can spend with my child?

4. What's important to my child? Is it important to me?

5. What practical steps can I take to make it more important?

6. When my child talks to me, do I really listen?

7. Am I setting goals? How can I help my child to set goals?

8. In what ways am I involved in my child's life each day?

9. Am I my child's biggest fan?

## PRAYER

*Heavenly Father, I know the time You've given me on this earth is precious. Forgive me for wasting time in worthless pursuits. Help me to find more ways to be involved in my child's life if I'm not involved enough. Am I hovering over my child too much? Forgive me, Lord, and teach me how to help my child become more independent. I want the things my child loves to be important to me. Show me ways we can discover more about her passion as a family. I want to be a better listener, Lord, and I want my child to feel she can safely express her hopes, fears, and deepest desires to me without fear of criticism. Let us be a family who sets measurable goals, and help us set the ones You would have us set. Let my child know I am and always will be her biggest fan and supporter. In Jesus's name, amen.*

# 7

# DESTINY OF THE DILIGENT

I N MATTHEW 25:29, the Bible says, "For to everyone who has, more will be given, and he will have abundance; but from him who does not have, even what he has will be taken away."

I love the way the *Spirit-Filled Life Bible* describes "have abundance":

> *Perisseuo*, Strong's 4052: To superabound, have in excess, greatly surpass, excel. The word shows the generosity of God's grace, giving assurance that faithful use of one's talents and gifts sets the stage for one's own advancement.[1]

I'm sure you've seen the "Life is Good" T-shirts with smiling Jake and the humorous sayings, but I bet you don't know how humble the beginnings were for this amazing company. Here's a little story I think illustrates the point of this chapter perfectly:

> In 1989 brothers Bert and John Jacobs designed their first T-shirts. They began selling their designs in the streets of Boston and out of an old van at colleges

and street fairs along the East Coast of the United States. While their intentions were good and their work ethic was strong, they knew nothing about the realities of such a business. As a result, it was not uncommon for them to live out of their van during road trips in their first five years, sleeping on top of stacks of T-shirts and subsisting largely on peanut butter and jelly sandwiches.

After five years in business, the brothers admit that they had "collected some good stories, but were not very prosperous." They persisted, searching for a unique brand that would capture the optimism they felt and their belief that there was room in the market for a positive message to counterbalance what they perceived as the heavy dose of negativity found in contemporary news reporting and media. In 1994, following a not-so-successful road trip, they returned to Boston, unsure of the future of their business. It was their common practice to gather friends at their apartment following such trips to share stories and to ask their friends to comment on drawings and sayings posted on their living room walls. In retrospect, the brothers realized that these were the first focus groups for their business.

On this occasion in 1994, one drawing received considerable favorable attention from their friends. The drawing was the head of a beret-wearing, smiling stick figure and the mantra "Life is good" together expressing simply everything the brothers believed in. They named the figure Jake and printed up 48 shirts bearing a smiling Jake and the words "Life is good." At a street fair in Cambridge, Massachusetts, the shirts sold out in less than an hour. With that, the

"Life is good" brand was born. The brothers began to sell T-shirts and hats featuring Jake in local stores. Demand for the merchandise grew quickly and has continued to grow in the succeeding years, as has national recognition of the brand.[2]

What a wonderful story! Hard work and diligence, patience and overcoming obstacles joined hands to create one of the greatest stories of business success in America in the last twenty years! Did you notice they labored consistently but with little success for five years? They never gave up but kept believing in what they were doing, even when there was little to show for it. Today the *Life is good* products are sold in more than forty-five hundred stores nationwide, and they are available in thirty countries.

> Do you see a man who excels in his work? He will stand before kings; he will not stand before unknown [obscure] men.
>
> —PROVERBS 22:29

## TEN THOUSAND—THE MAGIC NUMBER

Excellence and diligence breed success. In chapter 3 we discussed the research that revealed achieving mastery in any field can take ten thousand hours. The study cited was done in the early 1990s by psychologist K. Anders Ericsson and two colleagues at Berlin's prestigious Academy of Music, and it's fascinating what they found.

The professors took all the violinists at the academy and separated them into three distinct groups. One group had all the most talented musicians, the ones destined for a professional career as a world-class soloist. The next group contained the good but not great musicians, and the third group were those whose goal was to become a public school music teacher. They asked all of the violinists to come up with the number of hours they had actually practiced the violin from their very first lesson.

All of the students had begun playing around the same time at age five, and they found that all of them practiced around the same amount of time each week, two or three hours. By the time they were eight years old, a contrast began to surface, and the students who were deemed world class by the professors were already practicing more than six hours a week, eight hours a week by the time they were twelve, and sixteen hours a week by fourteen and onward until by twenty, they were purposefully investing thirty hours per week honing their skills on their instruments. By this time the world-class students had invested over ten thousand hours in their music career. The good students had invested about eight thousand hours, and the public school teachers, about four thousand hours each.[3]

What's really amazing about this study is researchers were not able to find any naturally gifted students who rose to the top without practicing as much as their peers. They also didn't find any students who worked harder than the others but just weren't good enough to make it. The basic conclusion showed that what "distinguishes one performer from another is how hard he or she works. That's it. And what's more, the people at the very top don't work just harder or even much harder than everyone else. They work much, much harder.... Practice isn't the thing you do once you're good. It's the thing you do that makes you good."[4]

For most of us, the opportunity to put ten thousand hours into anything is a pretty tough benchmark to reach on our own. It's a huge number, encompassing approximately ten years. But if you desire greatness for your child, know it happens only with incredible diligence, hours of practice, a financial investment, and a heaping serving of support and encouragement from you.

There really are no overnight sensations and no shortcuts. Talk to anyone who has reached the top of their field, and they will tell you it took years and years to get there.

When Franny eventually signed her record deal and broke into Christian music at the age of twenty-two, she was already a veteran performer. She had been on stage and involved in the performing arts since age four, gaining invaluable experience and logging thousands of hours of training and practice during those years. I haven't added up all the hours she devoted to working on her skills, but I would not be surprised to learn the number is extremely close to ten thousand. In the short three years since her first record was released, we have been humbled and gratified at the reception her music has received and the recognition she's earned. But to be perfectly honest, I had already seen a little glimpse of her future years earlier when, in faith, I called it out and spoke it over her.

## What Do You Model?

Whatever your hand finds to do, do it with all your might.

—Ecclesiastes 9:10

How hard do your children see you work at what *you* do? Are you setting an example of excellence in your household for them to emulate? What you do, they will follow, and the pace you set is the pace they will run at. My husband likes to say, "The speed of the leader is the speed of the group." If you sit at home during the day watching television or playing computer games for hours, you risk having your kids growing up to do exactly the same with their precious time.

Walking into one's destiny probably ought not to be called a "walk." In reality it can often be a strenuous climb. Success is not going to happen by accident, and successful adults don't just spontaneously coalesce! Most successful adults we know were raised to believe hard work and tenacious dedication are the pathway to success. The tangible rewards of financial, social, and spiritual success naturally follow the work needed to achieve them. To those who say success is a matter of luck, I offer the theory that the harder we work, the luckier we become. It's our job to set the example and to teach our children the value of diligence. What you model, they will follow.

## HONORING COMMITMENTS

Franny knew from an early age, if she committed to something, she would follow through! There was no other option in our house. She understood our respect for and our expectation of being on time to appointments and commitments. I'm sure she could repeat Mike's favorite adage about being on time verbatim. It goes, "If you're early, you're on time, and if you're on time, you're late. If you're late, then you might as well go home!" The gifts and talents God has given our children must be nurtured and trained. And to tell the truth, not all of those ten thousand hours will be happy hours! Sometimes you will feel as if you are pulling teeth to get them to do what they need to do.

I know my daughter didn't always want to practice or go to rehearsal or work on playing her guitar, but she will tell you today she is glad she did. In the doing of it, she formed the habit of diligence and developed a strong work ethic. In addition, she came to love the discipline and began sensing from God Himself a deep knowing what the calling on her life was all about.

We intentionally created an atmosphere in our house where her gifts were nurtured, celebrated, and honored, and we set high expectations. We set a standard of excellence in every area of our home life. She knew we wouldn't let her slack off in any area by modeling a job well done in our own work. We endeavored to exemplify daily, in large things and small, that anything worth doing is worth doing well and anything worth having is worth working for.

Franny knew growing up I loved to cook and entertain, and I tend to go all out when we have people over. I make pretty much everything I cook from scratch, and I have a passion for good food and making people feel special and welcome when they come to my house. It is such a passion for me that I started my own blog about a year ago to share my favorite recipes and cooking how-tos. So she knew, when we entertained, we weren't going to be cutting corners. We used the good china and the good silverware. We were going to be cooking, baking, cleaning, and all the other things it takes to entertain and offer hospitality. And she was going to help me! I knew I was setting an example for her not only in hospitality but also in taking the time to do things well and with excellence. As a wife and mom now, she is a gracious hostess who provides wonderful hospitality for her friends and family.

You know, what we are content to settle for is exactly what we'll get. Sadly, we all know too many families where the bar of expectation was set too low, and today, as young adults, the children are working low-paying, minimum-wage jobs with no real prospects for the future. Worse yet, they've not yet really grown up and haven't begun walking in the destiny God had planned for them before they were formed in their mother's womb. Working hard in school to get ready for college, learning a trade, or studying to serve in the ministry wasn't considered important enough, so it wasn't prepared for.

The path of least resistance might tempt us to allow our children to drift into adulthood rather than require them to take risks and possibly fail or suffer rejection. While not every child may be cut out for advanced college degrees or the life of a high-powered executive, failing to dig in to what God has planned for his life while you have time to help shape it can result in a less than fulfilling and happy future.

Have you noticed the increasing number of twenty-somethings still living at home, with few marketable skills, seemingly content to continue to drift into young adulthood with no deadline or expectation of when they will move out on their own? A side effect of the downturn in the economy has seen recent college graduates returning home in record numbers, sometimes with prospects for the future, but often with none. The term coined for these Generation Y emerging adults is "adultolescent." Another aptly named description is the Peter Pan syndrome, my personal favorite.

## What Is Adultolescence?

An adultolescent is basically a grown-up child living at home.

Life coach Christine Hassler speaks to this question in her column from *The Huffington Post* in this way:

> Labeling a rather non-conformist group within a generation is not new; take the Hippies of the Baby Boomer generation for example. However, adultolescence is unique to today's young adults due to the simple fact that now more than ever parents are financially supporting their twenty-somethings. According to the MacArthur Foundation's Network on Transitions to Adulthood and Bureau of Labor Statistics, parents provide, on average, $38,000 in material assistance for their child. That translates to about $2,200 given for every year between ages 18 and 34—considerably more than in the past. Some anti-Peter Pans use short-term fiscal support

to get on their feet while others take long layovers in Neverland. And more twenty-somethings are returning to the nest after college than ever before.[5]

Of course, not all twenty-somethings are in this category. Many are hardworking, responsible, and independent, but sadly, many aren't. And parents enable them.

She goes on to say:

> But there are some not so flattering characteristics that many (and I stress many, not all) members of your generation are exhibiting. A sense of entitlement and the desire for instant gratification that you mentioned is something that many members of the Gen X and Baby Boomer generations are noticing among twenty-somethings. Employers often complain about the lack of work ethic and grandiose expectations they see in young employees.[6]

If you have little ones, now is the time to start equipping them so that when they are out of school, they are beginning fruitful careers and making the most of their talents and gifting.

An article from *Newsweek* illustrates the adultolescent phenomenon quite well:

> When Silvia Geraci goes out to dinner with friends, she has a flash of anxiety when the check comes. She can pay her share—her parents give her enough money to cover all her expenses. It's just that others in her circle make their own money now. "I know I haven't earned what I have. It's been given to me," says Geraci, 22, who returned to her childhood home in suburban New York after graduating from

college last year. "It's like I'm stuck in an in-between
spot. Sometimes I wonder if I'm getting left behind."
Poised on the brink of what should be a bright future,
Geraci and millions like her face a thoroughly
modern truth: it's hard to feel like a Master of the
Universe when you're sleeping in your old twin bed.[7]

The "emerging adult" or adultolescent issue is a real phenomenon and a real problem in today's family. What then is
our response as Christian parents? John Piper, in his article
"A Church-Based Hope for 'Adultolescents'" from his website
DesiringGod.org, offers fifteen things he would like to see the
church do to combat what he sees happening in our culture. We
would do well to heed his advice.

1. The church will encourage maturity, not the
   opposite. "Do not be children in your thinking.
   Be infants in evil, but in your thinking be
   mature" (1 Cor. 14:20, ESV).

2. The church will press the fact that maturity is not
   a function of being out of school but is possible
   to develop while in school.

3. While celebrating the call to lifelong singleness,
   the church will not encourage those who don't
   have the call to wait till late in their twenties
   or thirties to marry, even if it means marrying
   while in school.

4. The church will foster flexibility in life through
   living by faith and resist the notion that learning
   to be professionally flexible must happen through
   a decade of experimentation.

5. The church will help parents prepare their youth for independent financial living by age twenty-two or sooner, where disabilities do not prevent.

6. The church will provide a stability and steadiness in life for young adults who find a significant identity there.

7. The church will provide inspiring, worldview-forming teaching week in and week out that will deepen the mature mind.

8. The church will provide a web of serious, maturing relationships.

9. The church will be a corporate communion of believers with God in His Word and His ordinances that provide a regular experience of universal significance.

10. The church will be a beacon of truth that helps young adults keep their bearings in the uncertainties of cultural fog and riptides.

11. The church will regularly sound the trumpet for young adults that Christ is Lord of their lives and that they are not dependent on mom and dad for ultimate guidance.

12. The church will provide leadership and service roles that call for the responsibility of maturity in the young adults who fill them.

13. The church will continually clarify and encourage a God-centered perspective on college and grad school and career development.

14. The church will lift up the incentives and values of chaste and holy singleness, as well as faithful and holy marriage.

15. The church will relentlessly extol the maturing and strengthening effects of the only infallible life charter for young adults, the Bible.[8]

He adds:

> In these ways, I pray that the Lord Jesus, through his church, will nurture a provocative and compelling cultural alternative among our "emerging adults." This counter-cultural band will have more stability, clearer identity, deeper wisdom, Christ-dependent flexibility, an orientation on the good of others not just themselves, a readiness to bear responsibility and not just demand rights, an expectation that they will suffer without returning evil for evil, an awareness that life is short and after that comes judgment, and a bent to defer gratification till heaven if necessary so as to do maximum good and not forfeit final joy in God.[9]

With the same vigilance we apply to helping our children maintain purity of heart and mind, we must face the realities of today's culture. We must strive to skillfully combat its influences, uncertainties, upheavals, and the shifts incessantly competing for our children. It's our responsibility to help them mature and grow with an eye toward an independent future, finding their way in the world separate from mom and dad.

I would love nothing more than my daughter to still live at home with me—all the more since her departure left us with a very empty nest. But for her to live the life God ordained before the foundation of the world, to discover His path and her destiny, it was necessary for her to leave home and make her own way as a young adult. There can certainly be extenuating circumstances, and things can happen out of an adult child's control. Parents will always help as best they can, but the danger lies in enabling the adultolescent to shirk personal responsibility for his future and rely on good ole mom and dad rather than grow up and learn to rely on himself.

Helping Franny pack, driving her to Nashville, and kissing her good-bye defied every maternal instinct in me at the time. As the mother of an only child, my heart wanted her to stay in Florida. But I knew God had been preparing us all for this very moment over the last twenty-two years. He gave me the peace of mind I needed to let her go and live her own life. This is what I'd prayed for! Her life wasn't with me and her father anymore. And it wasn't about me and my needs. Our goal must be to raise our children and then let them go (and sometimes give them the push they need) to live the life they have been called to live. And though it is difficult not to have her nearby, I know she is living the life God called her to and impacting many in her generation for Christ. My loss is the world's gain.

Our first job as parents ends in a sense and takes on a new dimension. We nurture and protect our children and equip them to face the world and live on their own. Our role changes significantly as our children grow up and move out. Although I sometimes selfishly wish to turn back time, launching our children into young adulthood is exactly what we're called to do as parents. And life goes on. For many, launching your kids (finally!) is when you might feel life actually begins. We're all wired differently, but for me, letting our daughter go to find her future on her own was the best thing we ever did for her and for us. Since she's been gone, I've started a blog, begun teaching home canning classes, and now, I've written a book. My life didn't end because Franny went out on her own, and neither will yours when the time comes to empty your nest and send the work of art that is your child into the future God has prepared for him!

## QUESTIONS TO ASK YOURSELF

1. Are you setting an example of excellence and diligence in your family?

2. Are you honoring your commitments? Do you require your children to honor theirs?

3. Have you set an atmosphere of high expectations for your children?

4. Do you have an "adultolescent" living in your home? How can you help him achieve independence in life?

5. Are you encouraging maturity in your child?

6. Are you willing to let your child go?

## PRAYER

*Lord, help me to be diligent in all I do. Let me be an example of excellence to my child in thought, word, and deed. Help me to set the bar high and to require my child to honor and follow through on his commitments. Show me how to encourage my child to grow and mature, and let me lead him to independence in life. I repent of making an idol of my child. Please forgive me and show me that my identity is not my child or my role as a parent, but my identity is in You.*

Being dedicated
in 1985

Seven months old
in our New York
apartment 1985

With dad in our Greenwich Village condo in New York; almost one year old

Enjoying an ice
cream cone!
About 2 years old

Daddy taught her to hang a spoon from her nose at about two years old!

Striking a
ballerina pose and
loving to dance

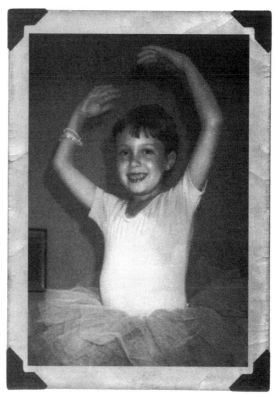

Littlest hula dancer!
four years old

First day at the Westerly
Learning Center
home-school coop
in Princeton, New
Jersey. Four years old

Crazy clown!
Six years old

My favorite picture! We had just moved to Florida, and Franny got her
hair cut for the first time—seven years old and pondering life.

Becoming a beautiful ballerina at age twelve.

First professional headshot by our good friend and master photographer Tim Kelly. Twelve years old

With mom at
another show
opening—twelve
years old.

Deep in thought after ballet class, around thirteen years old

Backstage with Franny at a performance of *The Bengal Tiger's Ball*, a children's musical written by and costarring Maureen Mcgovern— age thirteen

Backstage at *I Remember Mama*. Me as Mama, Franny as one of the children. She's around thirteen.

With mom and dad on opening night of *Ben-Hur: The Musical* in Orlando—fourteen years old.

In the TransCon Studios control room mixing an original recording—age sixteen

In the vocal booth
at age seventeen
(Tim Kelly photo)

At the indie music
conference in Las
Vegas where she
performed for her
peers for the first
time—2003

Mike and Kate—
Estes Park, Colorado

Franny and Kate at the Music in the Rockies event in Estes Park, Colorado, 2004

Packing up to leave Estes Park Music in the Rockies Conference with mom.

Casual photo shoot for Franny's independent release (photo by Crystal Cason), 2004

Her name in "lights"! One of the countless coffeehouse dates during the
independent artist years (with friend Laura Lathroum), 2005

One of the many Friday nights playing outside at Winter Park Village in Florida—around 2006

Promo shot by
Tim Kelly, 2007

With dad in Nashville when she first moved there in 2007

Signing her record deal with Fervent Records (Warner/Word), July 2007

In our backyard before Franny moved to Nashville—the good ole days!

A typical gig before moving to Nashville, selling her independent CD and earning tips!

# 8

# ENCOURAGING THEIR WALK WITH GOD

W E HAVE A pretty, handmade plaque hanging in our kitchen. I found it at a church craft fair years ago. It's made of wood in a half-moon shape with trees and a little house hand painted on it and these simple words from Joshua 24:15: "As for me and my house, we will serve the Lord."

That plaque has hung in our kitchen for more than twenty years as a reminder to me and everyone who visits our home who we are and what we believe. It's important people know where our family stands when it comes to our faith. And it was important our daughter knew it growing up. She knew it wasn't open to debate. As a family, we were determined to live our lives serving the Lord's purposes with our gifts, talents, and abilities. We also believed our role was to lead Franny, not the other way around! Too many families are child centered and allow their children to set the tone. A parent-centered home allows you to establish priorities and take the lead in decision making. Allowing the tail to wag the dog makes no more sense and bears no better fruit in your family than it does at the kennel club.

We unapologetically believe in the Bible. We've tried to live our lives based on God's simple, absolute truths, and we raised our daughter to understand what those truths are. We modeled our obedience to and our faith in God's Word in our daily lives, demonstrating our dependence on its foundation to absolutely guide us, guard us, inspire us, and delight us every day of our lives.

While raising our daughter, we believed it was our responsibility to teach her where her gifts and talents come from and what to do with them. When we moved to Orlando and out of the music and theater business, we continued to exercise our musical gifts in church. I sang, first with the choir, then as a member on the worship team. Mike played trumpet and assisted our worship leader however he could. Weeknight and early Sunday morning rehearsals were a sacrifice. Franny experienced some of that sacrifice firsthand by getting out of bed extra early and staying through multiple services on Sundays. She also witnessed the joy her parents felt in expressing themselves in worship with the gifts we used previously to make a living.

We believed it was our duty to teach her to value the gifts she was given and treat them as a sacred trust. I reminded her continually, "To whom much is given, much is required." (See Luke 12:48.) I'm sure I wore out that phrase when Franny lived at home, but it's become a foundational part of who she is. And she knows and deeply loves and respects the One who gave her the gifts and talents in the first place. She learned early on to seek the Giver, not the gifts. But she also learned she was going to have to work hard to develop the gifts God had given her. Ultimately she would spend years developing her gifts and honing her craft to become the artist she is today.

## BEING GOOD STEWARDS

We are responsible to take what God gives us and develop it into something worth presenting back to Him. I regard it as a form of worship to stand before Him and humbly offer back what He gave me, for His glory rather than my own. Learning to properly steward the gifts given us, to develop them and put them to good use, demonstrates how we value the trust God places in us by bestowing those abilities in the first place.

In the parable of the talents, Jesus teaches that He expects us to use and multiply what He gives us. They are *His* talents, not ours. I know this scripture is most often interpreted in a financial sense because it literally addresses a financial return on investment. But the lesson goes much deeper and applies to *every* area of life. When we value what God values and work hard to cause it to grow, we can happily expect to hear, "Well done, you upright (honorable, admirable) and faithful servant! You have been faithful and trustworthy over a little: I will put you in charge of much. Enter into and share the joy (the delight, the blessedness) which your master enjoys" (Matt. 25:23, AMP)

I believe it is incumbent on us as parents to help our children dig deep and mine the jewels of their gifts and talents. And it applies to our kids to be diligent and work hard to develop all God has given them. The consequences of shirking this responsibility are pretty harsh:

> But his Master answered him, You wicked and lazy and idle servant! Did you indeed know that I reap where I have not sowed and gather [grain] where I have not winnowed? Then you should have invested my money with the bankers, and at my coming I would have received what was my own with interest. So take the talent away from him and give it to the one who has the ten talents. For to everyone who has will more be given, and he will be furnished richly so that he will have an abundance; but from the one

who does not have, even what he does have will be
taken away.

—MATTHEW 25:26–29, AMP

Wow. Jesus calls us wicked and lazy and idle when we don't
give a return on His investment. But He commends those who
are faithful with their gifts. I don't know about you, but I
know what I want to hear when I meet Him someday! Muscles
atrophy if they're not used, and so will the gifts and talents He's
given us. And on top of that we stand to pay a steep price for
not honoring the Giver.

## THE POWER OF PRAYER

We'll be exploring the vital importance of prayer in chapter 11,
but because prayer is essential in encouraging our children's walk,
I believe it deserves a mention here. If there was one thing Mike
and I wanted to instill in Franny while she was growing up,
it was the importance and power of prayer. We prayed for her,
with her, one on one, as a family, together in church, for others'
needs, and for our family, country, and world. We prayed about
everything, anytime. We witnessed countless answers to prayer
that have encouraged our faith when the answers were positive
and caused us to seek Him more deeply when they weren't.

Prayer is simple but so effective. Nothing is too insignificant
to pray about. The primary purpose of prayer is to know God
better, not to have everything in my life work out perfectly. It's
easy to fall into the trap of making God the Father into a genie
in a bottle, which is not my attitude at all. However, the Word
reminds us, "Ye have not, because ye ask not" (James 4:2, KJV).
I believe in asking for all it's worth! He delights to give good
gifts to His precious children. And I've done my best to pass
this message along.

## IT'S ALL IN THE DETAILS

When I pray, I pray very specifically and in a very detailed way. When you take a close look at an oak leaf or a snowflake, you realize no two are exactly the same. One leaf will be shorter or greener or have a different veining pattern than the other. Each snowflake will have a singular shape and size. Amazing, isn't it? Everything God creates is unique down to the tiniest detail. God values the details in a leaf and in a life. I believe He wants to be involved in the tiniest details of our hopes, desires, and decisions both big and small. And I'm convinced it blesses His heart when we include Him in those details.

I write my prayers down and check them off when they're answered. And I write the date by the prayers in my journal when God answers them. I've done this for years. Oh, and I pray aloud and I pray Scripture whenever possible! Remember the power of words? The spoken word is the creative word. Every January I rewrite, in longhand not on the computer, prayers for my husband, myself, Franny, her husband, my grandson, friends, and family.

Two prayers were answered as I wrote this chapter this very week, and I excitedly checked them off my prayer list. First, Francesca's second CD, *Hundred More Years*, recently came out, and I have been praying for months it would debut at number one on the Billboard Christian chart. Why did I pray for that? Well, Billboard tracks sales and radio play, and it just makes sense to me that the more people who have the CD, the more chance some will come to know Christ or be drawn to God in some way. Fame for fame's sake has never been something our family valued. But fame for the opportunity to make God's name known and to have a bigger impact and larger platform *is* worth praying for.

I could have simply prayed, "God, let Francesca be famous

and let her sell lots of CDs." But to me, a prayer like that is too ambiguous and shows a lack of vision on my part. It also tends to sound like a typical prayerlike wish list passing for prayer for too many of us. I pray specifically because I believe He has great and quite specific plans for my daughter. And if He has great plans for *her,* He has great plans for *your* child as well.

## BE SPECIFIC IN PRAYER

God likes to give me specific things to pray for. When her first record had been out for about a year, God reminded me how I used to tell her she would win a Grammy someday and to begin praying again, specifically for her to be nominated for one in 2009. In my mind I was thinking, "She's a new artist. There's no way she would get a Grammy nomination." But He laid it on my heart in September, and because I like to think big, I wrote it down and began praying in earnest! I didn't tell anyone but my husband I was praying for this, but I prayed about it every day for the next three months.

Then, in December, Mike and I were watching the nomination telecast. About an hour and a half into the show, I felt prompted to get on the computer and see who the other nominees were. The live show was still on, but since only the top ten categories are announced on the broadcast, I knew I had to check the website. You might not be aware, but there are about seventy-five Grammy categories altogether.

I went to my computer and logged on to the Grammy website. I began scrolling down the nominee list past all the Latin, jazz, and classical categories, all the while holding my breath. Suddenly, I saw the category "Best Gospel Performance," and "Francesca Battistelli: Free to Be Me" was in the list of nominees. Mike was in the other room watching the telecast, so I shouted his name, yelling, "Mike, come here and tell me if this is real!" He came running in to see what the excitement was all about and to his delight saw our daughter's name as a Grammy-nominated artist. We were both just dumbfounded, yet thrilled and grateful beyond belief with her nomination. I wasn't surprised at all! Would she have been nominated if I hadn't prayed? I don't know, and it doesn't really matter. To me the experience was just another example of believing in and praying for big things and allowing God to expand my faith. God is sovereign, but He delights in including us in His plans! Franny didn't end up winning the Grammy, but she enjoyed the opportunity to attend the live show with her husband and walk the red carpet as a nominee.

The second prayer God answered concerned the Dove Award nominations this year. The Dove Awards are the Christian equivalent of the Grammy Awards. They honor excellence in all genres of Christian music. She won two Doves in 2010, one for Female Vocalist of the Year and the other for Short Form Video of the Year. I had been praying for at least one nomination for Female Vocalist again this year and hoping for a couple more. In mid-February the nominations came out, and she received four! I checked that off and wrote the date on my prayer list and reset my prayer for her to win a Dove. Is it important for her to win? Not in the grand scheme of things. She certainly doesn't need awards to know she is living her life's purpose and is valued and loved by the Father. But if it increases her impact on the kingdom of darkness, I'm going to pray about it.

Prayer update: At the time of this writing, her new record did in fact debut at number one on Billboard, and she won three Dove Awards from those four nominations.

## BE AN EXAMPLE

Let your children see and hear you pray. Let it become a daily habit. Rick made it a nightly ritual with his son when he was young, and now that he's grown, it's paying dividends:

> I was trying to get him to settle down for the night, but more importantly, it was a wonderful time for me to speak into his life and to spend time praying for him, but mostly, worshiping the God that I loved in front of him. I knew my actions would influence him more than anything else, but I wanted him to know the Lord the way I did. Most importantly, it was time that I enjoyed more than any other with him. I would lie down next to him and raise my hands in the air as we laid there on our backs and just start to worship the Lord. This was not practice for me. I love to worship God. I would speak my praises and start to thank Him for everything in our lives. "Lord, thank You for this home that we live in. Thank You for the roof over our heads and the cars that we have." I thanked the Lord for everything, including the wife he gave me and the mom my son had. I thanked God for our food and for everything we had. I would spend time just in thanksgiving for everything in our lives. What an honor, what a wonderful time it was for me because it was just me worshiping. This was not a performance, but the depth of my heart and my true feelings for all the Lord was to me. Now as an adult, I see him journaling and his life in Christ is entrenched in prayer, reading the Word, and following hard after the Lord! Somehow our children have to come to this knowledge of who God is. We are their avenue to know

what life in Christ is like. When we teach by example and do what we are called to do as parents, the Holy Spirit can bring His truth to them.

## CONTINUOUS AND CONTAGIOUS

Teaching our children about God and His love is a continuous process until they are grown and gone. And it's contagious once it starts. I love Deuteronomy 6:5–9. Jesus considered it the greatest commandment:

> You shall love the LORD your God with all your heart, with all your soul, and with all your strength. And these words which I command you today shall be in your heart. You shall teach them diligently to your children, and shall talk of them when you sit in your house, when you walk by the way, when you lie down, and when you rise up. You shall bind them as a sign on your hand, and they shall be as frontlets between your eyes. You shall write them on the doorposts of your house and on your gates.

In other words, pray when you're sitting around, walking around, and lying around, day in and day out, year after year. Love God and teach your children to love Him too.

My friend Carmen shares a beautiful illustration of the power of love and mercy through circumstances common to young people everywhere. She powerfully models Christ to her daughter in a canceled debt. Here's her touching testimony:

> We live in a cell phone era. So much so, that people are now foregoing landlines in their homes. And who would've ever thought the day would come when pay phones would look strange? Both of my

daughters have cell phones. Haley is seven years older than her younger sister, Abbey. So for Abbey, having a cell phone was commonplace. She began asking for a phone as early as elementary school. Being "mom," I thought she was still too young. Her Nana thought otherwise. So when Abbey's birthday rolled around, guess what she got from my mother for her birthday? I objected—but only slightly. I did see the merit in having it for safety, being able to get a hold of her quickly, etc. Plus, it was her birthday, and hands down her favorite gift.

As we had done with Haley, we told Abbey she could keep her phone with the understanding she would pay twenty-five dollars per month toward the bill. She did great—at first. She was falling further and further behind.

In the spring around Easter time, I had gotten aggravated with Abbey regarding money. I don't remember the specific reason, but as with most things, when you get mad about one thing, it quickly leads to another. So I pulled out the phone records and grabbed a blank sheet of paper. She had a few other debts that she owed, and I began to detail them on paper. I added up all the past due months that she owed us for the phone bill, pulled out the calculator, and began adding.

And that's when God spoke to my heart: "Carmen, cancel her debt. It's the Easter season; show her what it means to have her debt canceled because of what My Son did on the cross. For her. And for you."

Calling her by her first and middle name, Abigail Elizabeth, I asked her to come to my room. She rounded the corner thinking she was in trouble.

She wasn't. I asked her to sit down on the bed with me because I wanted to talk to her. The color immediately left her lips, and she began to shake. I tried to calm her as much as I could, but she knew something was up. I grabbed another sheet of blank paper and started the same exercise I'd just done, only this time with her watching.

I detailed all of her debt, line by line, month by month, dollar for dollar. With every "transgression" that I'd write, she began to shake a little more. She was getting the picture. By the time it was all said and done, she owed close to four hundred dollars—maybe even a little more. For a child not even in her teens, that was a huge number. She looked terrified, overwhelmed, and nervous. Seeing the fear in her eyes, I took the sheet of paper and ripped it in half. As I continued to rip the page, I said to my baby: "Abbey, Mommy is canceling your debt." She didn't understand. Nor did she fully believe me. So I explained.

"Sweetheart, you owe Mommy and Daddy a huge debt. A debt you cannot pay. But because we love you, we are canceling your debt. You don't owe us this money anymore. Accept the gift and be grateful. But Abbey, here's the real reason why I'm doing this today. Easter is in a few weeks. And this is what Easter is all about. God sent His only Son, Jesus, to cancel our debt—a debt we could not pay. Jesus canceled our debt by dying on the cross. His canceling our debt is a gift that He offers us. But you have to accept it."

For the first time in her beautiful blue eyes, I saw it click in her tender, young heart. I can't say that she accepted Jesus that afternoon, but a seed was firmly planted.

The Bible says in 3 John 4: "I have no greater joy than to hear that my children are walking in the truth" (NIV). As parents, teaching our children truth is not only our responsibility; it's our mandate. Growing great kids doesn't happen by accident. It only happens when we're intentional, honest, patient, and unwavering. And we must remember, God loves them even more than we do.

# MODEL IT

Our children imitate what they see us do. My daughter knows I pray, and when she has an issue in her life, she'll call or text me, confident I'll pray about whatever she's asked me. She knows I will because it's the pattern I set for her hundreds of times when she lived at home. Whenever there was a crisis, large or small, she knew prayer would be the first line of defense.

She also witnessed me reading my Bible, going to Bible studies, attending church, volunteering, attending conferences, and practicing hospitality. One of my greatest joys in life began as a simple morning routine once she became a teenager. Every morning she woke up to find me sitting on my favorite couch in the living room reading my Bible or doing Bible study homework. She would sit on the love seat across from me and open her Bible and read. Invariably Mike would join us, and we had our morning quiet time together as a family, and so many times we ended up having wonderful, deep conversations about God. I miss those times now that she's married with a family of her own, but I feel so blessed to have had them. I learned so much from her insights into the Word and loved hearing about the discoveries she was making and the revelation she was receiving. She developed a love for the Word and prayer because she saw love for the Word and prayer modeled. She learned to "seek first the kingdom of God and His righteousness, and all these things will be added to you" (Matt. 6:33) as we sought the Lord each morning before jumping into the busyness of each day.

## QUESTIONS TO THINK ABOUT

1. What are the absolutes in your house?

2. How are you stewarding the gifts and talents residing in your child?

3. How important is prayer in your family?

4. Do you talk about God when you're "sitting around, walking around, and lying around"?

5. What are you modeling?

## PRAYER

*Father in heaven, I know Your Word is truth, and it guides me, inspires me, and delights me. Help me to share this truth with my child. Enable me to teach her that her gifts and talents come from You alone. Give me the tools to guide her to develop them to the full. I pray she will become a good steward of the gifts and talents You've given her. Teach me how to pray specifically for my child. I know You care deeply about every detail of my child's life, and I trust You to show me how best to pray for her. I want to teach my child about You day in and day out so she knows You even better than I do. Help me to model to my child what I want her to become. Let me instill these words deeply into my child, "As for me and my house, we will serve the Lord."*

# 9

# MODEL HUMILITY

T HE WORD OF God is full of seemingly conflicting opposites. We are told to call those things that are not as though they are (Rom. 4:17). We learn the first will be last and the last first (Matt. 19:30; 20:16). We're told the foolish things of the world are what God uses to confound the wise (1 Cor. 1:27) and our strength is made perfect in weakness (2 Cor. 12:9). Labor to rest. And the greatest among you will be your servant (Matt. 20:27–28). And my personal favorite:

> Whoever exalts himself will be humbled, and he who humbles himself will be exalted.
> —MATTHEW 23:12

The world entices us to go down one road while the Word shows us a more excellent way. It's a low, narrow road, and few are able to find it. It's the road of humility, and humility is a classic mark of an authentic Christian. Christ modeled it throughout the New Testament:

> Learn from Me, for I am gentle and lowly in heart.
> —MATTHEW 11:29

Jesus...laid aside His garments, took a towel...
—JOHN 13:3–4

This is the same quality we are to model for our children.

The way of humility is the way of love. It's a low road and the only road. I am certain in this life the only way up is down. I'm convinced the degree to which you humble yourself is the degree to which you will be exalted. The lower you are willing to go, the higher He is able to take you. St. Augustine said, "Do you wish to rise? Begin by descending. You plan a tower that will pierce the clouds? Lay first the foundation of humility."[1]

Humility deals forcefully with our pride and our need to be seen and have our names known. It teaches us to make our lives others-focused rather than self-focused. It's the antithesis of pride, and if your desire is to be all He wants you to be, rest assured He will engineer experiences to teach you all about humility.

Jesus instructs, "Those who want to be great in the kingdom of God must be a servant of all." (See Matthew 20:26.) Greatness comes by serving others, by helping make their dreams come true.

It's important to consistently review your motives for your child and have them do the same for themselves. If God asked them to lay down their dreams for His purposes, could they do it? Would you *let* them do it, or are you too attached to their success because of how it will reflect on you?

Consider why God gave your child their gifts and talents in the first place. I believe there is one reason and one reason only: to bring glory and fame to His name—not ours. Sometimes a by-product of these gifts will be fame or personal glory, but these can never be the motive. Once achieved, you will find that fame can be a murky quicksand able to swallow you up in a heartbeat if you are not firmly grounded in godly principles.

If ever you find yourself thinking, "This is about me," you are headed on a collision course with not only humility but also most likely humiliation. If you don't believe me, check out what happened to King Nebuchadnezzar in Daniel 4!

## You Want to Do WHAT?

When Franny was a junior in college, a youth evangelist came to her youth group and greatly impacted the young people for ministry. He brought with him a team of interns who lived in community houses in Birmingham, Alabama. Together they traveled all over the country assisting him in his ministry. The interns took a semester or a year of their lives to serve him and support his vision of spreading the gospel to young people across the country.

By this time Franny had recorded her independent CD, was attending college full-time, and performed most weekends. She was super involved in church and serving the Lord with her gifts. But she started to get the itch to do something bigger, something scary and challenging and out of her comfort zone enough to cause her to grow. We like to call it taking a spiritual bungee jump! Franny had experienced our family's occasional ninety-degree turn in life, each one a spiritual bungee jump in obedience to what the Lord was calling us to do. She came to us after several weeks of praying and informed us she wanted to take a semester off from school, lay down her ambitions for music, and join the team of interns in Alabama.

Mike and I at first hoped this was a crazy idea that would soon pass. But we promised her we would pray about it, and as we did, we both felt it *was* the Lord's plan for her and we should support her desire to do it. We had apprehensions, but at the same time we felt peace knowing God had a purpose for all of it.

So off to Birmingham she went to a small, three-bedroom

house shared by thirteen young women. She went from her spacious bedroom and easy life as an only child in Florida to living in cramped quarters with twelve other girls, two bathrooms, and one refrigerator. Culture shock doesn't begin to describe it! Days were spent doing office work, Bible classes, and countless outreaches and road trips. She was deeply tested in many areas, yet at the same time her faith in the Lord grew by leaps and bounds. She learned many lessons, made new lifelong friends, and came back home changed and focused. The experience ignited her desire to serve God with her life more than ever, all while humbly working to serve someone else's vision.

I told her at the time her desire to put her plans on hold and go to Birmingham reminded me of Moses and the burning bush. The thing that has always struck me about Moses is how he made the simple decision to turn aside and look. He could have just passed by thinking it was a mirage, or he might have thought he was too tired or the heat of the desert had gotten to him and he was seeing things. Instead, he turned aside and looked, he paid attention to God—and it changed history.

I told her I felt she was doing a similar thing. She recognized God's burning passion in the evangelist and his mission, and she had to know more. Her hunger to see God work in power, to know Him better, and to make a difference with her life drove her to set aside all the comforts and security of home and spiritually bungee jump with both feet into an adventure, not knowing what would come of it.

Her willingness to lay down her future caused it to open up in ways none of us imagined. A year later she landed a record deal with a major label and moved to Nashville. When she went to Birmingham, she had no way of knowing what the future held, but she honored God in obedience, laid herself down, and He raised her up His way and in His time. Her courage to do it amazed me then and now.

## BIBLICAL EXAMPLES

Not everyone will be called to humble themselves in the same way, but they will be called to it in some way. Ruth shows us the way up is down. She abandoned her homeland and everything familiar to follow her mother-in-law, Naomi, to Israel. She humbly served and submitted to Naomi by gleaning in the fields and following her advice. She ended up marrying prosperous Boaz and having the great honor of being in the lineage of Christ. I don't think she ever imagined as a Moabite widow who left behind everything she had ever known what an amazing future God had in store for her.

Joseph is an example of a gifted individual with big dreams who learned humility the hard way. In his case he didn't humble himself voluntarily, but the lessons learned through slavery and imprisonment taught him it wasn't all about him. After years of unfair treatment and living in obscurity, Joseph learned the deep lesson of humility. God raised him up to greatness, and he was able to save his entire family and preserve the Jewish race.

Moses left behind his position, influence, and prosperity to watch over sheep for forty years. During his time in the desert, God so dealt with his pride that by the time God called him, he was reluctant to go and afraid to speak. God had to bring his brother, Aaron, along to be his mouthpiece!

John the Baptist made one of the most humility-filled statements in the Bible and one that strikes to the core of our pride: "He must increase, but I must decrease" (John 3:30).

In America especially, we mistakenly think it's about us: "I am, and there is none besides me" (Isa. 47:8). It's the cry of the world system surrounding us, and it infects every bit of our culture. As Christian families, we can model "a more excellent way."

## JUST CALL 1-800-HUMBLE-ME!

When she was about fourteen, Franny attended a local summer theater camp at the Orlando Shakespeare Festival. She loved acting and wanted to try her hand at classical Shakespeare.

By this time she had built quite an impressive résumé in musical theater. During the run of the camp, they put on a production of *As You Like It*. She eagerly auditioned for one of the lead roles. With all her experience, she expected to land a great part.

When the cast was announced, she was given only a small part. Her ego was bruised and her spirit was downcast. But since they knew she could sing, they were going to write a song for her. We talked about it, and I encouraged her to take the part and give it 100 percent. I reminded her how God will test us to see what's inside. And usually the form these tests take will strike right at the heart of our pride. Mike likes to say, "We don't know what's in us until we get stepped on and we see what comes squishing out!" It was a humbling experience for her, but she stayed the course and found joy in the process of putting on a show and making relationships. When opening night came around, she performed with grace and professionalism and was thrilled to have her singing prominently featured. Suffice it to say, she learned more about humility than she did about acting that summer.

We used to joke about making up T-shirts saying, "Just call 1-800-HUMBLE-ME," because during those years we all had so many opportunities to take the low road. But I continually reminded her God can only raise you up to the degree you let Him humble you. The lower you go, the higher He'll take you.

I see it as an undeniable principle in God's Word. What's so powerful about it is the more you humble yourself, the more like Christ you become. The attachments of the world become far less attractive as He becomes more and more real. It becomes easier and easier to give your place to someone else and be content where He has you. I think one of the reasons God has lifted Franny up in Christian music is because success as defined by the world wasn't what she was seeking. Yes, she wanted to make music and be involved in the arts, but fame and fortune weren't her goals. Her passion was and still is Christ and making His name known. The upshot is He has made her name known and given her a platform to spread the gospel far beyond her dreams.

## SERVE YOUR CHILDREN

As parents, our joy in life is to serve our children. We endure sleepless nights, defer our dreams, and devote our finances to provide our children opportunities to grow, thrive, and find their purpose. And we don't think twice about it. Our selfish desires fall by the wayside (hopefully) when we become parents. We will gladly sacrifice and do without so our children won't have to, and we gladly rearrange our priorities as the need arises.

We humble ourselves day in and day out, pouring out our lives to raise up the next generation of world changers. We do it because it's what parents do! It's the model that Christ gave us in giving His very life for us. Motivated by love, He laid down everything in order that through Him we could have access to all the riches of heaven. Love inflamed by passion for Christ will impact our kids more than anything else we can give them. Help them learn to humble themselves. It doesn't come naturally to any of us, but it's a solid principle just like sowing and reaping. In fact, the more you sow in humility, the greater chance God can trust you with His dreams!

We have wonderful pastors who have raised four great boys. Pastor Ron and Sandy Johnson are terrific models of integrity, humility, and godliness. They are authentic and down-to-earth people whose lives are great examples of loving God and loving people. We're blessed to call them friends and benefit from their years of wisdom in raising their family. They did a wonderful job conveying these virtues to their boys.

> We tried to show our four sons, not just tell them, that being humble doesn't mean walking around with your head down or feeling that you're worthless. Rather, it is a mind-set of gratitude for what God has given us, a realization that every human being deserves respect because they are a work of the Creator, and living a life of generosity toward people.
>
> While in high school, Jordan, our firstborn, worked at the Ralph Lauren/Polo Outlet. He was able to get some great clothes for himself at great prices. However, on more than one occasion, he came home from school without the new sweater or shirt he had worn that morning. When I asked what had happened, his answer usually went something like this: "Mom, there's a guy in my math class that doesn't ever have any good clothes on. He told me he liked my sweater, so I gave it to him." Now, as a grown man and a business owner, when Jordan sees a guy with a "Will Work for Food" sign, he stops and offers to employ him for a day to help him out, or takes him to a local restaurant to feed him. Reaching out to others who are needy expresses humility.

How do you express humility to your children? When you get passed over for a promotion at work, do they hear you complaining about your boss and denigrating your coworkers? Or do they see you praying for those who hurt you, and do you assure your children God still has an excellent plan for your life?

What do they see or hear when the family is driving somewhere together and the car in front of you cuts you off? Have you ever made a mistake and had to ask forgiveness from your child? This is where the rubber meets the road for Christian parents. We all can talk a good talk about God, but how do we handle ourselves when we're treated unfairly? Or told to wait? Or told no? Or told we're not good enough? We all face these things, and so will our children. They will react as they see us react. Teach your children well.

## QUESTIONS TO THINK ABOUT

1. How do you model humility in your family?

2. If God asked your child to lay down his dreams would you let him?

3. How could you serve your children better?

4. When you face a humbling experience, how do you handle it?

## PRAYER

*Father, humbly I come into Your presence and acknowledge Your sovereignty. I ask You to show me the areas in my life where I need to learn humility. Show me it's not about me, but it's about me bringing glory and fame to Your holy name. Give me the strength to take the low road and to model Christlike humility in my family and my life. Teach me to serve and be an example of one who desires You above my hopes and dreams. Let humility mark my life.*

# 10

# WHEN YOUR CEILING
# BECOMES THEIR FLOOR

G IFTS AND TALENTS often run in families. Throughout history, family businesses, ideas, talents, and passions have been handed down through the generations to children and grandchildren to be carried on or carried further. Some of these businesses remain small family-run enterprises, virtually unchanged from generation to generation yet preserving the heritage and the original intent of the founders. Businesses abound like the corner grocer, the local family-owned restaurant, or the rancher who continues on in the family tradition of raising cattle on the land of his father and grandfather.

Other family businesses go on to become industry leaders, infinitely more successful, larger, and further reaching than envisioned by the founders. Companies such as H. J. Heinz, whose founding dates back to 1869 and is still run by the family today, or the SC Johnson company begun in 1882 and currently run by a fifth-generation descendant. Other examples of multigenerational family companies include the Trump Organization, the Disney Company, Levi Strauss, and the Ford Motor Company.

A quick look in the field of entertainment and you find the Osmond family, rap music pioneer Master P and his son Lil'

Romeo, Judy Garland and daughter Liza Minnelli, Will Smith and son Jaden, actress Blythe Danner and Academy Award–winning daughter Gwyneth Paltrow, Kirk Douglas and son Michael Douglas, Lloyd Bridges and his Academy Award–winning son, Jeff Bridges.

In everyday life, many sons and daughters continue their father's or mother's legacy. Sometimes God will take what began with you and distill, amplify, and expand it in your child. Mike and I are gifted musically, and so is our daughter. Before Franny was born, we experienced significant success in our chosen fields—music, acting, conducting, recording, and musical theater. We didn't fully achieve all of our goals, but we worked consistently. We were on an upward trajectory and were considered by our peers to be quite successful in our field. My heartfelt desire during those years was to be a thriving, Tony Award–winning Broadway star whose name was synonymous with "leading lady." Mike had equally lofty goals beyond his accomplishments of conducting orchestras for Broadway, national tours, and Radio City Music Hall.

So there we were living and working in New York City, newly married, successful, happy, and what happens next? We met the Lord, and He turned everything in our lives upside down! As brand-new believers we prayed for wisdom and for ears to hear God's will for our lives and careers. We were surprised when God seemed to make it quite clear He had a different plan for our lives and future. What did we hear? Only the most difficult thing possible for two young career-oriented, success-addicted, limelight-seeking musical theater professionals could hear: lay down your dreams of continuing your careers and leave New York and your Broadway aspirations behind.

We struggled with this for a while and then found we were also having a baby! This was, of course, exciting, wonderful news that changed our paradigm considerably. It was right around the same time that I was offered the starring role in a South African production of *The King and I*, which was planned to have a six-month run. When I turned down the role, I told the producer I couldn't do it. After all, I was pregnant (not to mention this was at the height of apartheid, which I was completely opposed to). His response? "Oh, don't worry; we have great midwives in South Africa." He didn't get it, didn't take no for an answer, and applied even more pressure by upping the stakes and offering me more money! Needless to say, I didn't go to South Africa!

We began to earnestly pray about a number of life's questions. We loved our careers and we loved New York, but we also had dreams of a large family and wondered if we really wanted to raise our children in the city. We prayed about what to do with our careers and all the years we'd invested in building them. We were still baby Christians and didn't really know how to hear from God, so of course we sought counsel and prayer. One night during this time we turned on the television to watch a Christian preacher. There was great music, a wonderful message, and then came his altar call. During this passionate appeal for changed lives, it seemed like he pointed right at us through the television and practically yelled, "You actors and actresses who think you can straddle both worlds! You need to come out from that life and give yourselves fully to God. Come out from among them and be separate!" We looked at each other, stunned and wide-eyed, believing God was speaking right to us. While we weren't in the habit of making life-changing decisions based on what we saw on television, it certainly contributed to our eventual heartfelt conviction to leave the business, leave New York, and make a significant ninety-degree turn. Don't you love how dramatic God can sometimes be? We prayed through our first major life decision as young marrieds, got our answer, and carved out a new future for ourselves.

We had our baby girl, sold our condo in Greenwich Village, and moved to Princeton, New Jersey, and eventually Orlando. We exchanged our lofty dreams of fame and fortune for home-schooling, homemade jam, and a home-based business. We walked away from our dreams in obedience not fully under-standing God's plan at the time. However, deep in our hearts, we had the divine assurance we were making the right choice.

I think God knew that for us, as brand-new believers, the temptations facing us in the performing world would be too much for us to handle. It's all too easy to compromise your convictions when money and fame are involved. While still living in New York, I would get regular audition opportuni-ties for soap opera and movie roles. But many of the parts my agents were sending me for compromised my newfound faith. In His wisdom, God took us clean out of the business and the temptations residing in the performing arts world. We moved away with our little girl, planted a vegetable garden, and didn't look back. At first, we did move only forty-five minutes from Broadway just in case God changed His mind!

## GOD's ECONOMY

Even though we changed course and laid down our careers, we knew the call on our lives to music and the arts had not been lifted. Mike has a doctorate in music, for goodness sake, and I had spent more than a decade doing dozens of shows, concerts, and television. I firmly believe God's gifts and callings are irrevocable. Though we weren't sure how it would manifest at the time, we soon learned God's economy is never wasteful. If you've been trained in an area God might require you to lay down, I believe the time will come and circumstances will arise for the training and experience to be put to use again in some way. It's possible those gifts will be used in ways quite different from your original plan, but if you're patient, God will often bring them back around. And that's just what He did!

As young parents, we had early signals Franny's gifts might be similar to ours. So we enrolled her in ballet at age four to see if it suited her. She completely adored ballet and seemed to have a real gift for dance. She was also drawn to music and drama at an early age. We definitely didn't want to force her down any particular career path at such a young age. We believed since we had an aptitude for the arts, it made sense that she might just follow in our footsteps—and we were right. She gravitated more toward the arts than sports and loved creative writing more than math or science. We continued to support her interests, involving her more and more in dance, theater, and music as the years passed. Through a series of events, God led her more deeply into music and songwriting, and she developed a full-blown passion for it as she matured.

We allowed the seed of our desires to die and go into the ground. They laid dormant there for many years before bearing fruit in Francesca's life. All the desires we laid down, all the unfulfilled dreams we had for ourselves, God has more than fulfilled through her. We could only take our dreams so far. We laid them down, but God redeemed them and has given them kingdom purpose in our daughter's career. She's taken it much further than we ever dreamed.

Because of our years of training and experience, we were able to guide her in the early days. We knew the dedication it took to achieve excellence in the arts firsthand, and because of that we were able to steer her to the threshold of a professional career in music. God had a much bigger purpose in mind for our arts training than our fame and fortune. He took what we laid down, distilled it, and refined it in her life. Now, she's running with it to the next generation. It's every bit as satisfying, in fact more so, to see your child raised up and being a role model to others and making music that's blessing so many lives.

Once we knew her calling and she demonstrated a passion and a willingness to be diligent in her gifting and to work hard, we were able to call on our training and begin to pour into her all our knowledge and expertise. Mike managed her career in every aspect by finding opportunities to play, negotiating for her, buying and setting up her equipment, financing an independent album for her to sell, and accompanying her to countless gigs wherever there was an open door to play and sing. We taught her the value of setting goals, working hard, and honoring commitments. I shared all I knew about performing, staging, and preparation, and I helped her develop good habits she still draws on today.

## SHE'S NOT A MINI-ME

Mike and I were especially aware we could easily influence our daughter to become the conduit to our unfulfilled dreams. Admittedly, every year in June when the Tony Awards are on TV, we watch with wistfulness for our former life and wonder about what might have been. Would we have achieved real success in New York? Would I have starred in a Broadway show conducted by Mike? Could we have been on TV accepting a Tony or Emmy Award? Maybe. But then, we had the distinct thrill of being in the audience at this year's Dove Awards and were privileged to watch as our daughter's name was announced three times winning three awards, including Female Vocalist of the Year and the prestigious Artist of the Year!

Just last month, we both burst into tears the first time we sat in a darkened movie theater and heard her song being played on the soundtrack of the major motion picture *Soul Surfer*. We wouldn't trade moments like those for anything in the world! I believe God will be faithful to take what we lay down in obedience and raise it up in the proper way in His perfect time.

> Most assuredly, I say to you, unless a grain of wheat falls into the ground and dies, it remains alone; but if it dies, it produces much grain.
>
> —JOHN 12:24

We were content to let our dream die and see it bear much fruit in Franny's life.

Our desire was to pour into Franny the best of our knowledge and experience. But our challenge was letting her find her own unique expression of her gift. As much as we were passionate about musical theater, we couldn't let our preconception of success shape her future. We knew she had to find her own way, and we trusted God had a unique plan for her, different from the plan He had for us.

However, we know it isn't the same in all families. What do you do when your child doesn't share your gifts and talents, and she can take or leave the things that bring you the greatest joy? I'll let my friend Robert's words give you some perspective:

> One of the difficult things for us as parents was to try to differentiate between God's gifting in our son and our personal aspirations for him. I am a musician and loved playing musical instruments. Because this was my gifting, I desired for this to be his gifting as well. I would have loved for him to pursue the same direction and have the same passions and interests.
>
> As a lot of parents do, we gave our son piano lessons. We discovered although he enjoyed music, he truly had no interest in learning to play the piano. We attempted this with multiple instruments,

and still no inclination, gifting, or desire. I realized this created a lot of frustration for him and a little resentment too. My wife and I had several conversations concerning whether we should "force" him to continue. We came to a realization that even if this was something we greatly desired for him, we had to recognize it was not a desire or gifting of his.

I had to relinquish the thought of making my son like me, but allow him to be who he is supposed to be and not who I desired him to be. There is freedom in this and a total rightness about it. I remember writing a dedication to him and saying, "You be you!" As his mother and father, we had to learn how to let him be who he was supposed to be and not who we wanted him to be.

As long as we have instilled in our children the righteousness that comes from knowing God, and not trying to be God, then we can rest in the fact that the Holy Spirit really does teach all things and will completely direct their paths in a way that will cause them, without effort, to live lives of great effect in the world.

## He Takes Away the First to Establish the Second

In the Book of Hebrews the writer says, "He takes away the first that He may establish the second" (Heb. 10:9).

This passage is talking about the daily temple sacrifices, but I believe it applies to our situation as well. What God began in Mike and me, He has established in our daughter and our ceiling has become her floor.

It's an interesting principle in the Word how God always

seems to choose the second person. Isaac instead of Ishmael. Jacob rather than Esau. David, not Saul. Ephraim over Manasseh. Christ, not Adam. First Corinthians 15:44–46 states, "There is a natural body, and there is a spiritual body. And so it is written, 'The first man Adam became a living being.' The last Adam became a life-giving spirit. However, the spiritual is not first, but the natural and afterward the spiritual."

In our case, we came to the Lord later in life, and our careers were rooted in the natural world with natural goals and ambitions. We brought up our daughter to pursue the kingdom first and had faith to see where God would take her. Now He is using her in the field of music to have a far greater impact than we were ever able to have. He is allowing her to achieve what was only a dream for us. He took away the first to establish the second. This may not be true for every family, but it's been our experience. Our ceiling has become her floor.

## QUESTIONS TO THINK ABOUT

1. What gifts, talents, and abilities run in your family?

2. Are they evident in your child?

3. Has God called you to lay down something you love?

4. Are you willing to use what you've laid down to help your child reach success in her field?

5. Are you letting your unfulfilled dreams control your child's future?

# PRAYER

*Father, first of all, I'm so thankful for the gifts and talents I've inherited from my family. I'm grateful for all You've deposited in me, my spouse, and my child. I see so much in my child, and I'm excited about the future. Please help me to recognize her unique gifts and talents, and give me the wisdom to guide her as she develops those gifts. Help me to recognize if I'm letting my unfulfilled dreams get in the way of my child's future. Don't let me impose anything on her that's not from You. Let my ceiling become my child's floor, and let her life be a testimony to You.*

# 11

# PRAYER, THE ESSENTIAL INGREDIENT

N OTHING WILL BEAR more fruit in your child's life than prayer. Volumes have been written on prayer with deep insight and wisdom. I don't need to tell you why to pray for your children, and I'm certain you already do. But I can share what Mike and I have learned about prayer and how we still pray for our daughter today. If I convey only one vital truth in this book, I hope it's the need to be a praying parent. Time on our knees is the best investment we can make in anyone's life...especially our children.

A friend of mine was divorced when her three daughters were young children, and she raised them as a single mom for many years. She is now happily remarried to a wonderful, godly man. Her circumstances have taught her how to press in to God in prayer, and she has learned some powerful lessons:

> Prayer has been the most significant exercise of my faith. Spending time on your knees, crying out to God without ceasing, is the richest and most rewarding place you can be. I have prayed for each of my daughter's salvation before they were born. I

have prayed that they would come to know the joy of the Lord through worship and have prayed for the Lord's protection and blessing over their lives. The Word says, "'Let the little children come to Me'" (Matt. 19:14). Parenthood is a combination of joy and challenge and can best be approached by believing and persevering in prayer for your children. I am confident that it was prayer that birthed our daughters and has sustained them. Over the years, each has watched us pray and seen our prayers answered. Today, because of prayer, a generational blessing and legacy has been established for our daughters and grandchildren. It's all for God's glory.

## Big God Dreams

Before Creation, before the foundation of the world, before he was a glimmer in your eye, God knew your child and set a plan for his life story firmly in place. God ordered his every step and set the course for every twist and turn of his life. He dreamed a big dream and gave you the task, with His help, of discovering what that big dream is. He wants to guide you every step of the way and help you dig down deep and mine every ounce of greatness in your children. The dreams and desires we hold for our children and for ourselves are so important to God—more than we can even imagine.

I've never been afraid to believe God had a huge plan for my daughter's life. I was just naive enough to take God at His Word and believe in the power of destiny. I may not have always believed it for myself, but I had no problem believing it for her. And I have seen my belief bear tremendous fruit over the years. Don't be afraid to dream BIG for your child.

## PRAY THE WORD

Nothing is more powerful than the Word of God. The Word is alive; it's the sword of the Spirit, and it will not return void. God spoke the universe into existence with a word. In Genesis 1:3, "God *said*, 'Let there be light, and there was light" (emphasis added). Isaiah 55:10–11 says, "For as the rain comes down, and the snow from heaven, and do not return there, but water the earth, and make it bring forth and bud, that it may give seed to the sower and bread to the eater, so shall My word be that goes forth from My mouth; it shall not return to Me void, but it shall accomplish what I please, and it shall prosper in the thing for which I sent it."

The Word is the seed (Luke 8:11), the source of all life and growth on earth. When Jesus spoke to Satan, He said to him three times, "It is written..." He intimately knew the power of God's Word!

The book *Prayers That Avail Much* by Germaine Copeland has inspired me to pray Scripture when I pray. Reading it motivated me and taught me how to pray specific scriptures when interceding for friends or family members. I learned my prayers do, in fact, avail much, not because of my holiness or worth in God's eyes (I know my righteousness is as filthy rags), but because the Word of God is all-powerful. They're His words, not mine. I'm simply agreeing with God and praying His words back to Him.

I don't always pray Scripture, but sometimes just heartfelt words from the depth of my soul. Or at times, when God has specifically shown me something to pray about, I simply follow His lead and speak out what I believe He is instructing me to pray. Other times, when I truly don't know what to say, the Holy Spirit will make intercession "with groanings which cannot be uttered" (Rom. 8:26).

I encourage you to pray what you see in your heart even if it seems impossible. "Faith is the substance of things hoped for, the evidence of things not seen" (Heb. 11:1). I think God puts those impossible dreams, those "things not seen," in our hearts for the very reason that they are impossible without His divine help and intervention. I know that without Him, I can do nothing. But with Him, absolutely nothing is impossible!

I've learned to pray big, bold, audacious prayers. We have not because we ask not. I mean, who prays for a Grammy nomination or a number-one spot on Billboard? God has shown me too many times it's not about me; it's about His purpose being manifest on the earth. I'm convinced a lot of the things that have happened in Francesca's life are the result of prayer, not just my prayers but hers as well. She would tell you prayer is essential in her life.

## They Are Watching

Our children watch what we do, and they want to know if we are doing what we are telling them to do. My friend Adrianne learned this lesson well:

> If our children were going to live a life of prayer, it had to start with us. As parents we had to be the example. We couldn't just talk the talk, but we had to walk the walk because, believe me when I say, they were definitely watching, watching to see if we lived what we said, walked what we believed. It was in prayer we consecrated our children to the Lord, which wasn't an easy thing to do because that meant we had to turn them loose, meaning our plans and purpose for them may not be what God had for them. We had to choose to dedicate them for God's

purpose, trust Him, and devote ourselves to raise godly children so that they could become the man and woman of God He called them to be.

## DECREE AND DECLARE

> You will also declare a thing, and it will be established for you; so light will shine on your ways.
>
> —JOB 22:28

*Decree* is defined as an order, usually having the force of law. To *declare* means to make known formally, officially, or explicitly. To *proclaim* is to declare publicly, typically insistently, proudly, or defiantly and in either speech or writing. God gives each of us the power to proclaim, decree, and declare. Remember what Proverbs 18:21 says, "Life and death are in the power of the tongue." What we say and what we pray have a huge impact on the world around us. Because the Word does not return to Him void, everything we say, every word we speak is heavy with power.

For a long time I've decreed and declared what I believe God was saying to me. But first I had to believe it in order to decree it—and I had to speak it out loud. Did you know that the word *spoke* or *speak* is used more than fourteen hundred times in the King James Version of the Bible? I'm not suggesting whatever we decree God is obligated to fulfill. We need to use wisdom in praying. We can decree a Cadillac in our driveway till we're breathless and blue in the face, and I can guarantee it's not going to magically appear! But when we are in agreement with God's will, when we know a thing to be true, when we are calling those things that are not as though they are, we will see results in prayer. The key is, we must know God's will and what God's Word says.

When I do this, I typically declare Bible promises. For

example, I might say, "Lord, I declare Francesca is blessed and highly favored. She's blessed coming in, and she's blessed going out. She is the head and not the tail. She is above and not beneath. She is growing every day in wisdom and stature and in favor with You and man." I could go on and on with Bible promises, but you get the point. I believe it's important to pray out loud for your children whenever possible. Imagine how encouraging it would be to your own faith to hear life-affirming words from Scripture being prayed for you. It would make you feel strong and invincible and that anything was possible. Faith comes by hearing and hearing by the Word of God (Rom. 10:17). I believe in proactive, preemptive prayer. We create reality with our prayer by coming into agreement with God's will in a situation.

I've learned to be bold in prayer. "Let us therefore come boldly to the throne of grace, that we may obtain mercy and find grace to help in time of need" (Heb. 4:16). When it comes to our kids, boldness is essential in every area. We need to be bold with their teachers, bold with their friends, bold in our family witness, bold in protecting them, bold in our role as parents, and bold in authority. Additionally, we must be bold to believe in our children's future. We had audacious faith to believe God's Word that He had a future and a hope for our daughter. And Franny has audacious faith too. Here's a tremendous illustration of her faith.

## STANDING IN FAITH FOR THE IMPOSSIBLE

When Franny was a young teen, she was diagnosed with scoliosis, or curvature of the spine. She was seen by both a chiropractor and an orthopedic specialist. She experienced a serious growth spurt that exacerbated her condition, and the treatment she received didn't help it improve. When she was sixteen, a top

Orlando orthopedic surgeon scheduled her for a spinal fusion using metal implants or Harrington rods, a serious and invasive surgery with a long recovery period. The procedure involves cutting you open from your neck to your pelvis, inserting metal rods through your spine, and fusing the vertebrae to keep your spine straight. Surgery doesn't by any means cure the condition, but it typically removes or improves the curvature and helps you to be able to stand straight.

We learned all we could about the surgery and scheduled her for the following January. Needless to say, we all prayed and sought prayer for the healing of her condition and for wisdom from God. We wanted to be certain we were on the right path, since any kind of surgery is risky and this one particularly so as it involved the spine. The procedure would take hours to perform with months of postoperative recovery.

A week before the surgery we were scheduled to give blood so she would have her own available during the procedure. If they needed extra blood, they would be able to use her blood rather than a stranger's. As I hung up the phone after making the appointment, Franny came to Mike and me with a serious look on her face. She told us she'd been praying and felt the Lord telling her He was going to heal her and she was not to do the surgery after all. We were shocked and frightened and excited all at once. As parents, we want our children to make bold choices, to take a fearless stand for faith, and to press in and hear God for themselves. At least we say we do. When they actually step out in bold faith, let me tell you, it can be the scariest thing in the world—and in this case it was!

Mike and I had to stand back, assess the situation, and measure the impact of this audacious decision on our daughter's life. If we stood in the way and didn't allow her to make this decision, we feared she might not have an opportunity to exercise her faith with so much at stake again. Scoliosis is not a life-threatening condition, but it can be disfiguring and cause pain and possibly compromise one's internal organs in the future. Even though her condition wasn't life threatening, it was serious. Surgery is a medical option many choose, and at the time we were comfortable with it—at least as comfortable as we could be with our daughter facing major surgery.

We've always prayed for Franny to be a woman with fearless faith, as we knew she would need it in the field she was entering. After praying about this decision as a family and receiving peace from the Lord, we let her know we were in agreement—no surgery. I called the doctor's office to cancel the surgery, and, as you can imagine, he was not pleased and tried to dissuade us. It's difficult to make a decision that flies in the face of medical opinion and stand in faith for the impossible. And we're still standing.

As of today in 2011, nine years later, she has not yet received her healing. I still fully believe in and am standing firm on God's promise of healing. He alone makes "the crooked places straight" (Isa. 45:2), and like everything else I've believed for her life, I've seen it in my heart long before I've seen it in the natural. We ask God (and keep asking) for Franny's healing and know one day our faith will become fact. Meanwhile, she has bold faith that's been made bolder by her decision to believe for something the doctors say is impossible. Backs don't straighten on their own. But with God, nothing is impossible!

People often say, "I'll believe it when I see it," when in fact it ought to be the other way around. God has shown me over the years that when I see it (in my inner man with my spiritual eyes), I'll then be able to believe it. And when I truly believe something is typically when I actually then see it. It's always been that way for me. I see it first or sense it from the Lord, pray about it, believe it, and then see it come to pass. Experience has shown me time and time again that "I'll see it when I believe it"!

Mike and I were and still are very proud of the difficult decision she made. She has pain from time to time, can't do everything she'd like to do, and often tires easily. Because of scoliosis, her dream of a career in dance came to an end. But when God closed that door, He opened another in music. And scoliosis seemingly hasn't slowed her down at all. She's been able to tour extensively and carry a pregnancy to term. I'm excited to see how God will bring about her healing one day. No matter what, Francesca loves God for who He is and not just for what He does for her.

## BE SPECIFIC IN PRAYER

God is a God of details. His creativity is endless and knows no bounds. He is specific and intentional in creation. How many blades of grass, snowflakes, fingerprints, or galaxies exist, and not one of them exactly like another? He cares about every detail of life, even the little things. He knows when a sparrow falls to the ground and dies (Matt. 10:29), and He knows every thought you think, every dream in your heart, every breath you take.

I learned a long time ago if I was going to take the time to pray, I would be detailed in my prayers—not long-winded, but detailed and specific. I am convinced God cares about my life. I have a neighbor who disagrees with me about this. He thinks God has more important things to do (like solve world hunger) than to be concerned with our day-to-day troubles. I disagree totally, believing God knows everything about me and delights to be invited into every area of my life.

I know this because He tells us in Psalm 139:1–4:

> O Lord, you have searched me and known me. You know my sitting down and my rising up; You understand my thought afar off. You comprehend my path

and my lying down, and are acquainted with all my ways. For there is not a word on my tongue, but behold, O LORD, You know it altogether.

He goes on to say in verses 13–18:

For You formed my inward parts; You covered me in my mother's womb. I will praise You, for I am fearfully and wonderfully made; marvelous are Your works, and that my soul knows very well. My frame was not hidden from You, when I was made in secret, and skillfully wrought in the lowest parts of the earth. Your eyes saw my substance, being yet unformed. And in Your book they all were written, the days fashioned for me, when as yet there were none of them. How precious also are Your thoughts to me, O God! How great is the sum of them! If I should count them, they would be more in number than the sand; when I awake, I am still with You.

How amazing that the thoughts God thinks toward you and me are more in number than the sand! I think you'll agree He is in the details! And because of that, I pray detailed prayers— sometimes *very* detailed prayers. When Franny was in school, I specifically prayed about all her classes and for her teachers. Even when she was in college, I prayed for wisdom for her in choosing classes, for her professors, and for her to be diligent in her work and have enough time to complete all her assignments.

Today, as I learn what tour is being planned or where she's headed for each different engagement, I pray specifically for a long list of things. I pray for safe travel, for her ministry to impact many each night, for energy and good health, for good accommodations, and much more. You get the idea. I even pray for parking spots for myself. Yup, I'm one of those Christians! Sometimes I get good ones and sometimes I don't. But I learned a long time ago, you don't get what you don't ask for. Or as God says, "You do not have because you do not ask" (James 4:2). Are you afraid to ask? I'm not! And I come boldly before the throne of grace to present my requests to God—because He tells me too!

So let me encourage you: Pray audacious, impossible, detailed, big (and small), bold prayers. God is a big God. He can handle it. And if you are praying outside His will, He will show you.

## CONSISTENCY IS KEY

I love the way the Amplified Bible translates Matthew 7:7–8. It says, "Keep on asking and it will be given you; keep on seeking and you will find; keep on knocking [reverently] and [the door] will be opened to you. For everyone who keeps on asking receives; and he who keeps on seeking finds; and to him who keeps on knocking, [the door] will be opened."

Prevail in prayer. Keep asking until you get the answer! Sometimes I say to God, "OK, it's me. I'm like that woman who kept bugging the unrighteous judge (Luke 18:1–8). I'm going to keep bugging You until I get an answer from You. Yes or no, I need an answer, and I won't give up until I get one!"

The Amplified Bible says it this way, from James 5:16, "The earnest (heartfelt, continued) prayer of a righteous man makes tremendous power available [dynamic in its working]." We need to be continuous and consistent in prayer. And the good thing is, God tells us to!

## WRITE IT DOWN

I pray for a thing until the grace for it lifts or until it's answered. I like to write down the answers to prayer and date them. I love to look back and see the history of God's faithfulness in my life. It's so encouraging to read through my old prayer requests and reflect on what God has done in our family's life. His history of faithfulness is my testimony and is the very reason I'm writing this book in the first place. He's taught me so much about who He is over the years, and He's shown me my life matters. So does yours. And especially, so does your child's—because he is the future.

## SHORT-TERM OR LONG-TERM?

I've prayed for some things for years, such as Francesca's healing from scoliosis. Other things I've just begun praying for. At the beginning of each year, I am in the habit of writing down my basic prayers, reviewing those that been answered, and renewing those yet to be answered. Of course, my written prayer is dynamic—a living, breathing document, being added to and with check marks, dates, and often how God answered my prayers.

At the start of this year, I prayed for Dove nominations, and when she received four, I wrote it down and dated it. Then I began praying she would win one, and when she won three, I wrote that down and dated it. When she was younger, I would pray specifically about her schooling and for wisdom each year as to what classes she should take. I'd pray always with an eye toward the future, mindful of what was going to best prepare her for college.

When Franny was a little girl, we started to pray a very long-term prayer and began praying for her husband. Mike and I would sit on the end of her bed before she went to sleep at night and ask the Lord to raise up a young man who would keep himself pure for her, who loved his parents, who loved and honored the Lord, and who would love, marry, and provide for our daughter and treat her with love and respect. We asked God to bless him and, when the time was right, to bring him into her life. Our prayers were answered more than twenty years after we began to pray this prayer in the form of our son-in-law, Matthew, who does truly love God and love his family. And he adores Franny and treats her like a queen! God so honored Franny to give her a man who was raised in a wonderful Christian home by wonderful godly parents. He is a tremendous husband to our daughter and is a fantastic father to our grandson, Matthew Elijah, and we couldn't have asked for more! My advice? It's never too early to start praying for your child's future spouse.

I also began to pray for my future grandchildren years ago. Even before Franny had any hint marriage was near, I began to pray in earnest for her children. I firmly believe the next generation is destined to change the world. They are also likely to inherit a world heading into its darkest days, and I felt strongly it was time to start. My primary prayer for them is that they love and serve God all the days of their lives. I pray and firmly believe they will be world changers. I pray for excellent health, strong minds, gifts and talents, and the opportunity to put those gifts to use in ways to serve God and change lives. I pray about everything! No detail is too small and no idea is too big to scare me away. God has challenged my faith over the years by prompting me to pray for big things—and He's answered those big, impossible prayers time after time in my life.

When Franny first moved to Nashville and her career began heating up, I sensed the enormity of what was coming for her and felt inadequate to handle it myself. God laid it on my heart to contact the women in my circle who knew Franny in some capacity and ask them to become part of a prayer team for her. I knew she had a real need to be covered in prayer because of all the traveling she was doing. Also, I was aware the more visible she became and the higher the Lord took her, the bigger the target she would be to the enemy. I reached out to the ladies and invited them to join me. Every month or so for several years now I send out a request for prayer in specific areas and include praise reports and answers to earlier prayer requests. I'm so blessed these ladies have helped to share the burden with me.

How great would it be to organize a group of moms or dads you know and respect and begin praying for each others' children? Prayer is such a powerful but sometimes underutilized tool in our arsenal. Coming into agreement with another parent for her child's needs is an amazing opportunity for fellowship, accountability, and possibly life-changing answers to prayer in your own family. God will often reveal things to others in prayer you may have overlooked or are not able to recognize on your own.

## THE FATHER'S BLESSING

In the Old Testament, it was the tradition for fathers to bless the sons, and when the father prayed, his words came to pass. Always! Noah cursed Canaan and blessed Shem (Gen. 9:25–27). Isaac blessed Jacob (Gen. 27:27–29; 28:3–5). Jacob blessed Joseph's sons in Genesis 48:12–20 and blessed his own sons in Genesis 49. The ancients understood the power of both blessing and cursing, especially when spoken with authority. Do you recall how upset Esau was when he found he'd been cheated of his father's blessing? He cried, "'Have you only one blessing, my father? Bless me—me also, O my father!' And Esau lifted up his voice and wept" (Gen. 27:38). He knew only too well what his father prayed would come to pass.

In traditional Jewish homes today, the parents will often bless the children on Friday evening when they celebrate the Sabbath. They lay their hands on their children's heads and pronounce a traditional scriptural blessing. It's a beautiful tradition, and the good news is, you don't have to be Jewish to bless your children—and you don't have to wait until Friday night! We regularly spoke blessing into Franny's life and still do so today.

When she got married, we had a beautiful time of prayer where each of the fathers came up and prayed publicly for their children before they said their vows. Mike prayed this beautiful prayer chock-full of blessings, knowing that what he prayed God will bring to pass.

*Franny and Matt, I bless you with overflowing peace and fruitfulness.*

*I bless you with* success *in everything you put your hands to, and* I release excellence *as the standard in everything you do because of who you are in God and who God is in you.*

*I bless you with* health and strength *of body, soul, and spirit.*

*I bless you with* overflowing prosperity, *enabling you to be a blessing to others, AND that you live generously by doing all to the glory of God.*

*I bless you with* spiritual influence, *for you are the light of the world and the salt of the earth.*

*I bless you with* abounding love *as you minister God's love and grace to others.*

*I bless you with the spirit of* wisdom *and revelation.*

*And I pray that you continue to grow in* wisdom *and* stature *and in* favor *with God and man.*

*You are blessed, Francesca and Matthew, with all spiritual blessings in Christ Jesus.*

*It is said that when children find* true *love,* parents find *true joy. Here's to your joy and ours, from this day forward, in the name of Jesus. Amen.*

One of my favorite scriptures in the Bible is the Aaronic blessing from Numbers 6:24–26 (NIV):

The LORD bless you and keep you; the LORD make his face shine upon you, and be gracious to you; the LORD turn his face toward you and give you peace.

What a simple but powerful prayer you can pray anytime for your loved ones.

I encourage you to pray without ceasing, call those things that are not as though they are, and come boldly before the throne of grace. Be specific, write your prayers down, and date and document answered prayer. You will see results. I promise!

## QUESTIONS TO THINK ABOUT

1. What big God dreams do you have for your child?

2. Do you pray what's in your heart, even when it seems impossible?

3. Do you pray out loud for your child?

4. How can you make your prayers more detailed and specific?

5. Do you keep asking, seeking, and knocking, or do you give up too soon?

6. What long-term prayers are you praying?

7. Do you write your prayers down?

8. What answers to prayer have you experienced in your family?

# PRAYER

*Father, I come to You in the name of Jesus. My heartfelt cry is that You would teach me how to pray! Your Word says if we lack wisdom to ask You for it and You'll give it liberally and without reproach. Give me divine wisdom in prayer. Show me what to pray and teach me how to pray. Put a big dream in my heart for my child. Teach me how to decree and declare Your Word. Remind me to be specific and consistent in my prayer time and begin to show me what long-term prayers I should be praying. Thank You, Father. Amen.*

# 12

# GROWING INTEGRITY

M Y FAVORITE QUOTE about integrity boils it down to its essence and goes like this: "Integrity is doing the right thing even if no one is watching." Or as my friend Brittany says, "Right is right, when no one is doing it, and wrong is wrong even if everyone is doing it." Socrates said, "The first key to greatness is to be in reality what we appear to be." And Billy Graham says, "Integrity is the glue that holds our way of life together. We must constantly strive to keep our integrity intact. When wealth is lost, nothing is lost; when health is lost, something is lost; when character is lost, all is lost."[1]

Nowadays, kids are taught to do whatever they need to get ahead, and worldly success has become our god. The pressure is on to get into a good school and get a well-paying job. Cheating is rampant in schools and colleges and has risen dramatically in the past fifty years. Coaches teach athletes how to fake injuries and make illegal moves, and they imply by their behavior that winning the game is more important than playing by the rules. College students convince doctors to prescribe Ritalin and Adderall to help them focus and get a better grade when they take exams. They don't actually have attention deficit disorder but claim they do in order to get the prescription. Did you know there are websites where students can download a research paper and call it their own?

Movie stars cheat on their spouses and have babies out of wedlock with no consequences to their careers. Politicians take illegal campaign donations, and when they get caught, they simply pay it back with little or no backlash. We had a president who debated the definition of what *is* is. Just in the last few months it was revealed that Arnold Schwarzenegger fathered a child out of wedlock with an employee who lived in his house. John Edwards was indicted and may now go to jail for improper use of campaign funds to cover up an affair and illicit love child. Anthony Weiner resigned from Congress for twittering unsavory photos of himself and then lying about it.

Are you the person you tell your kids you are? Do you do what you say you're going to do and follow through on promises and commitments? Do you do the right thing even when no one is watching? The truth is, children model what we *do* and not what we say we do. Actions really do speak louder than words when it comes to integrity. Integrity is doing the right thing when no one is looking. But integrity is also doing the right thing when the pressure is on and *everyone* is looking.

My friend Adrianne, a seasoned prayer warrior and wonderful wife, mom, and grandmother, offers these words of wisdom:

> Our kids learned very early that keeping a good name and maintaining respectable character had to be a foundation in their lives. We are known and called by our name, and they needed to understand when someone calls their name what comes to that person's mind. We go through life putting our names on just about everything. How we live our lives is important to God; it's important to our family and

friends. When our life is over on this earth, what will others say about us? We wanted them to know how critical this is. When they gave their word to someone, they had to keep it. How they handle their money would show their integrity, how they treat their parents, what kind of friend they are. Do they show up on time? Do they do what they say they are going to do? Do they live by moral and ethical principles? Are they honest? How can we ever hope our children will live a life of integrity if we as their parents haven't done our best to set the example?

Integrity is the foundation of trust, and it's an essential ingredient of true leadership. After all, who wants to follow a leader they don't trust? The dictionary provides three definitions for *integrity*:

1. Firm adherence to a code of especially moral or artistic values

2. An unimpaired condition

3. The quality or state of being complete or undivided

This last definition reminds me of the scripture, "He is a double-minded man, unstable in all his ways" (James 1:8).

## Modeling Integrity

How do you teach integrity? Well, you can try to teach it, but the best way to teach integrity is to model it—and it's best to start in early childhood. I recommend removing the words "Do as I say and not as I do" from our vocabulary. As Christians we know our hearts are exceedingly deceitful. In fact, Scripture says in Jeremiah 17:9, "The heart is deceitful above all things, and desperately wicked; who can know it?" Any mother of a two-year-old can tell you that! Because of our sin nature, we know the propensity to lie resides deep in our DNA. Every little one will lie first until it is trained out of them. It can come as quite a shock the first time it happens. "Not my perfect angel," we think. That is, until the cookies are missing, the crumbs are all over her face, and she boldly says she didn't eat the cookies; it was somebody else! By our actions, our children have to know they can trust us.

Franny is blessed to have a wonderful husband and godly in-laws. Annabeth and Billy Goodwin raised three children who are all passionately serving and following the Lord, and I believe the example of integrity they set for their children throughout their lives is one of the reasons why. Here are some words of wisdom from Annabeth:

> This was a recurring theme in our practice of instilling important character traits in our children. They saw us do what we were teaching them. Don't get me wrong; they also saw us lose our tempers occasionally or make a mistake on something, but then they heard us apologize and try to make amends. That in itself was a teaching moment. We weren't perfect by any means, but felt our example was as important a teaching tool as our words. Choosing to not have alcohol, smoking, or drugs in our lives taught our children those things weren't necessary for a happy, fulfilled life. Showing them we loved each other, as well as them, gave them an example for their own future spouses. Driving the speed limit and paying our taxes without trying to "cheat" the government reinforced the teaching of obeying the law. Watching

how we talked about and worked with others taught them respect, commitment, and loyalty. All of these traits are necessary to truly be a person of integrity.

Knowing we were seeking God's guidance in raising our children gave us hope that we were doing the right things. Watching our children wait for the spouses God had for them was a big answer to our prayers. And now watching them raise their own children brings back so many of these memories. When our daughter, Joy, as an adult, told us she learned more from our example than lectures, I breathed a sigh of relief. Seeing Matt grow and develop his incredibly compassionate heart has really made me smile. Hearing our son Will, who has recently become a pastor, use some of these lessons as sermon illustrations is a very real blessing. "I have no greater joy than to hear that my children are walking in the truth" (3 John 4, NIV).

I've known parents who let their children lie for them. They have them say, "Mommy's not home," to someone on the phone when they are standing right there. They let the children hear them call in sick when they are perfectly healthy. If you are ever tempted to think they're not watching and listening to every word you say or no one will ever find out, resist the temptation! Your kids will respect you and learn so much more when you do the right thing.

We model integrity by keeping our promises, keeping our word, and following through on our commitments. Our children need to see our word as our bond and know that we can be trusted to follow through. They need to see us do what we say we are going to do, for them and for others. Franny grew up knowing if we committed to do something, we were going to follow through, and so was she!

## DOING THE RIGHT THING, EVEN WHEN IT COSTS YOU

When our daughter was young and we had been in Florida only a few years, we built and operated a thriving business in the telecommunications field. As market conditions changed and consolidation in the telecom industry seriously hurt our business, we were faced with a difficult decision. The choices were to either honor the financial commitments we'd made to our clients and partners, or declare business bankruptcy, preserve our capital, and force creditors to come after us. For some in business, the decision to accept bankruptcy protection would have been a no-brainer. In fact, the advice we received from our CPA and attorney was to do just that. For us, however, following the conventional business wisdom being offered just didn't feel right, and we didn't have peace about it. We were painfully aware of the practical and financial consequences, but after praying about it, we knew we had to bite the bullet and do the right thing. We kept the business open while we wound it down and ultimately paid out tens of thousands of dollars, taking out a second mortgage on our home to fulfill our obligations to our partners. This was an extremely difficult time financially, but we eventually made our way back onto solid financial footing. It was not only the right thing to do, but it was also a tangible life lesson.

Making this decision as a family was a great teaching moment and spoke volumes to our daughter. She learned that sometimes doing the right thing is the hard thing, with consequences affecting the whole family. We went through a season where we had to tighten our belts quite a bit, but she saw the Lord redeem our decision, and business success followed. We took it on the chin for a few years, but we were able to sleep at night knowing we had acted with financial integrity. We took joy in being able to tangibly demonstrate God's influence in making a difficult life decision. In the end God restored everything and more when we followed the path He directed us to take.

This story from Sandy, the wife of our pastor, vividly illustrates this principle:

> As parents, Ron and I tried to not leave to chance our sons knowing the right thing. We frequently used life situations that came up as an opportunity to intentionally teach them scriptural principles. As pastors, believe me, there are always lots of examples, both positive and negative, to draw from! Unfortunately, there have been many times when people, even those in ministry, showed lack of integrity by not keeping their word or by making choices incongruent with who they claimed to be. We would discuss these situations with our boys, pointing out the hurt it caused not only the person himself, but also their family and the body of Christ.
>
> Right out of college, our second son, Justin, had a great job. He enjoyed the job and was well suited to it. However, he began seeing inconsistencies in what he knew to be right and what he was asked to do. He called his dad and me for counsel and decided to fast and pray to make sure he was seeing things correctly. Then he humbly made an appeal to his boss to not require him to do some of the things he was instructed to do that he felt was a compromise to his beliefs. The appeal was rebuffed, and Justin made

the decision to resign the job. Humility is expressed in integrity.

## STANDING ALONE

A mark of true integrity is having the courage to stand alone, against the tide. Francesca's alma mater is the University of Central Florida. With her theater background, she initially chose to major in musical theater. She applied, auditioned for, and was accepted to the BFA musical theater program—a highly respected and sought-after degree program open to only a handful of freshmen each year. Being one of those chosen was an accomplishment in itself and quite a feather in her cap. Little did she know, her integrity would be deeply tested her very first week of college.

The university's theater department held auditions twice a year for the shows they would be producing on their various stages during each semester. The year Franny was a freshman, there was one musical and several straight plays planned for the fall semester. The musical was a Stephen Sondheim piece called *Assassins*. It's an interesting but quite dark and violent musical revue about the various men and women who throughout history attempted to assassinate United States presidents—not your typical romantic comedy. As a freshman, she didn't think she had a prayer at getting cast in the musical since typically, the roles in musicals, especially lead roles, went to upperclassmen. When the callbacks were posted, she was called back for the lead role of Squeaky Fromme, a young woman who attempted to assassinate President Gerald Ford.

Franny quickly arrived at a crossroads, facing the choice between doing what she knew to be the right thing or doing whatever it took to get ahead in the program. She looked at the script and saw her character used extremely foul language and acted in a very sexually suggestive manner. Being part of this production and cast in that particular role was innately unacceptable to her, so she decided she would not do the show.

The only way out was to meet with the imposing head of the theater department to tell him she simply could not take on such a role—pretty scary thing for a brand-new freshmen. She was quite aware what an honor it was to be called back at all, and she knew taking herself out of the running could have serious consequences for the rest of the year, if not the remaining four years. But playing this role would cause her to compromise everything she believed in.

She was honest with him and let him know that portraying the character of Squeaky Fromme went against everything she believed in and she needed to be pulled from the running. Thankfully, he was gracious and released her. Interestingly, just months later she was cast in a major spring production in a role created for her where she could play her guitar and sing! This lesson was almost custom tailored to reinforce following her conscience and doing the right thing. She honored God, and He honored her taking a stand for integrity.

At the end of the first year, when deciding what classes to take for the following year, she felt God prompting her to consider changing her major and to focus on her music career. In the university's musical theater BFA program, there was little time for anything else, including being able to pursue music or play out anywhere during her first year on campus. More and more she was feeling God's tug to dig into her gifting and pursue music with a greater focus. So back she went to the head of the department, this time to tell him she was leaving the program. She believed it really wasn't fair for her to take a spot in such a highly coveted program when there were so many students who desperately wanted her place. She loved musical theater, but it wasn't her overriding passion and she didn't believe it was her calling. So she gave up her spot and became a creative writing major. It was a trying experience, but she learned to trust her heart, to listen to God's promptings, to pray through, to stand up for what she believed, and to trust that God would be with her every step of the way.

There are so many important character traits for parents to model to their children, including honesty, courage, respect for others, perseverance, humility, patience, fairness, compassion, and responsibility. I believe all of these naturally follow if we model integrity in thought, word, and deed as our foundation. Teaching, modeling, and instilling integrity as a requisite value when they are young can save our kids from making bad decisions later on when the stakes are so much higher.

## DON'T DO WHAT I DID

It's not always easy to keep our word or to follow through. It's not always convenient to drive the speed limit! In fact, driving the speed limit is probably one area where I fell down on the job of parenting. I am guilty of inadvertently teaching my daughter to drive like me. Now, don't get me wrong. I'm a good driver, but I drive just a little too fast sometimes. I can also be impatient with other drivers on the road, especially when they're on their phone and not paying attention. I've been known to honk a time or two when I probably shouldn't have. I tried to teach her not to do as I do, but to *do* as I *said*—which as you can guess didn't work so well. In all honesty, though, Franny is a great driver and has gotten only one speeding ticket. I, on the other hand, have been through traffic school three times! I do find it interesting that Franny writes and sings about having "dents in my fender"[2] after backing into a lawyer's car and doing "45 in a 35,"[3] both lyrics from number-one songs! It's good to know God can redeem those times when we fail to set the very best of parental examples. Thank God!

## COMMITMENTS

Throughout her growing up years, we gave our daughter ample opportunities to see us choose integrity with finances in big and small ways. If the cashier at the supermarket happened to make an error and give me too much change, I would go back to the register with Franny in tow to make it right, even if we had left the store. As a family we made a conscious decision to be scrupulously honest with our finances, to not fudge on our taxes, not take income under the table, not incur careless debt, and to pay our bills on time. If we made a commitment to do something for someone, we followed through. We made a decision and determined as a family not to attend R-rated movies, and we didn't.

We also determined to teach her to respect and honor the commitments she made, even when it wasn't convenient. During those early years as an independent artist, Mike would do the booking for Franny to play a gig. We made a family decision to accept any offer to perform within driving distance from home, whether it was for a large festival or a coffee shop at the crossroads of nowhere—and there were plenty of the latter. Missing a date, making an excuse, being late, or not showing up just wasn't an option unless, of course, she was really sick.

In addition to learning to honor commitments, Mike booked her to perform under every condition imaginable, from 95 degree Florida heat to freezing cold Friday nights outdoors with an electric heater at her feet and fingerless gloves on her hands. The experience served her well in so many ways, and to this day, almost nothing can throw her off balance when it comes to performing under combat conditions.

183

One particular festival performance was near a very large lake on a blustery spring day about an hour from home. It was a chilly day and quite windy on the festival grounds. On the stage adjacent to the lake the winds were blowing at what seemed like gale force. And it was cold with the wind off the water. There were probably only eight or ten brave souls in the pavilion to hear her set, including the friends who came with us that day. It was so windy, we literally had to anchor her to the stage! Nonetheless, like the postman's creed, "Neither snow nor rain nor heat nor gloom of night" would keep her from her appointed performance! She learned the lesson well, and today she pushes through the obstacles facing her and honors her commitments.

I remember another time when a performance we booked conflicted with a girls' church retreat she really wanted to attend. She had committed to both but was unaware at the time they were going to overlap. The girls' retreat began on Friday, and she had a gig Saturday night. When she realized the conflict, she was not a happy camper. Her first choice was to cancel the gig. We did not agree, and because she was still living at home, we required her to leave the retreat early and honor her commitment. She was not at all happy about it (or with us), but she knew there were simply some areas we wouldn't let slide. So she did the gig, and it actually turned out to be really good. When it was over and we were driving home, she was glad she hadn't missed it and thanked us for reminding her how important it was to "let your 'Yes' be 'Yes,' and your 'No,' 'No'" (Matt. 5:37), and then stick with it.

# QUESTIONS TO THINK ABOUT

1. What does integrity mean to you?

2. How do you feel about cheating? Is it ever justified?

3. How do you model integrity to your children?

4. Are you willing to do the right thing even if it means standing alone?

5. Are you willing to do the right thing even when it means financial hardship?

6. Do you honor your commitments and require your children to as well?

# PRAYER

*Father, I know that my heart is deceitful above all things and desperately wicked. I want more than anything to live a life that pleases You and to be a good example to my children. I want my yes to be yes and my no to be no. Help me to walk in integrity every day when I'm being watched and when I'm alone. I want to be an example to my children with my finances, my words, my job, and my commitments. Holy Spirit, bring conviction where necessary and bring truth and light to my mind. Forgive me for past mistakes and help me walk each day as an example of honor and integrity. In Jesus's holy name, amen.*

# 13

# TIMING IS EVERYTHING

W HILE RAISING OUR daughter, we learned a lot about discerning God's seasons. In life we will walk through many different seasons, and knowing how to recognize which one we are in is critical in continuing to press into God's purpose for our lives.

> To everything there is a season, and a time for every
> purpose under heaven.
> —ECCLESIASTES 3:1

Strong's translates *season* in the above scripture as "an appointed occasion—season, time."[1] So "To everything there is an *appointed time*" is speaking of a process, events happening in an orderly fashion appointed by God in the wisdom of His will.

There are multiple seasons mentioned in Ecclesiastes. The author mentions twenty-eight different seasons in these few passages. No wonder it seems like things are always changing in our lives! When I read this scripture, I marvel at God's marvelous plan and providence in His appointed times for our lives:

To everything there is a season, a time for every purpose under heaven: A time to be born, and a time
to die; a time to plant, and a time to pluck what is
planted; a time to kill, and a time to heal; a time
to break down, and a time to build up; a time to
weep, and a time to laugh; a time to mourn, and a
time to dance; a time to cast away stones, and a time
to gather stones; a time to embrace, and a time to
refrain from embracing; a time to gain, and a time
to lose; a time to keep, and a time to throw away; a
time to tear, and a time to sew; a time to keep silence,
and a time to speak; a time to love, and a time to
hate; a time of war, and a time of peace.

—ECCLESIASTES 3:1–8

He goes on in verse 11 to say, "He has made everything
beautiful in its time." As we simply "do life," we get to experience
firsthand many, if not all, of these twenty-eight seasons. Life is
fluid and ever changing. Just when you've grown accustomed
to the heat of summer, the whisper of fall is in the air and the
leaves begin to change and the nights turn cool. As parents,
each season brings new joys and new challenges to understand
and contend with.

You can be certain of this—just when you have a handle on
one season, it will change! Some seasons last longer than others,
and some go by quickly. Some will cause you to grow, and some
will require that you put into practice what you learned in the
previous season. Life may, in fact, let you leapfrog over certain
seasons in their entirety. In my child-rearing experience I have
been able to identify ten different and distinct seasons. These seasons are by no means definitive but simply what we've observed
and experienced over the years. They include the seasons of

growth, preparation, maturity, multiplication, disappointment, humility, chastening, failure, success, and acceptance.

## SEASONS OF GROWTH

From the moment your child is born, he is growing—first infant, then toddler, next a little child, then school age, adolescence, teen, and finally young adult and beyond. The season of growth will encompass most, if not all, of the other seasons. This is the time when your child is learning and becoming the person God has called him to be. The extent to which your child, with your help and guidance, learns to navigate the various seasons of his life determines how well rounded and well grounded an adult he will eventually become. An adult who has succeeded in learning from and growing through the inevitable seasons of life isn't always immediately recognizable in a crowd. One who has not, however, often sticks out like a sore thumb.

## SEASONS OF PREPARATION

Proverbs 24:27 says it best: "Prepare your work outside; get everything ready for yourself in the field, and after that build your house" (ESV).

The season of preparation includes all the years of your child's schooling and training as you dig down deep to mine the precious jewels of his calling. If your child is to become one of Malcolm Gladwell's outliers, now is the time the ten-thousand-hour clock begins to tick. If you have a child who is a gifted future pianist, the ten thousand hours begins with those first piano lessons. The future prima ballerina begins her ten-thousand-hour journey the day she first slips on a leotard and goes to ballet class with her hair in a bun. The future major league pitcher is working diligently perfecting his skills in Little League during this season. The next NBA star is diligently running drills and practicing free throws for count-less hours after school and after dark.

The season of preparation can run concurrently with several other seasons and, for true world changers, will last most of their lives. Francesca began taking dance at four, was taking voice lessons, acting classes, and doing professional theater at eleven, and began playing guitar and writing songs at sixteen. By eighteen, she had produced her first independent album and was being invited out to play regularly.

My friend Linda has raised two lovely daughters with her husband, and both are diligently pursuing God's plan for their lives. She shares this story about the seasons in the life of her older daughter:

> Learning to navigate the different seasons of your child's life is one of the most challenging yet impor-tant skills to cultivate as a parent. For me, I found the key to achieving this is simply listening to the Holy Spirit, then obeying what He says.
>
> One such time in my oldest daughter's life was when she was in eighth grade. Up to this point in her life, she had been homeschooled and was attending a really good Christian school. She had many friends and did very well in school, but like most middle schoolers she struggled with insecurity and self-image. It was during her eighth grade year God began to speak to my heart about putting her in public high school. To my natural mind, I found this thought shocking and scary because our local high school did not have a good reputation. Uprooting her from her safe Christian school and taking her away from all of her wonderful friends seemed like it would be traumatic for her. But in the depths of my heart, I

had been crying out for my children to really know God and not just know about Him. And as many of you know, when God is speaking He will not give you peace until you obey Him. So after about six months of praying and stalling, she was registered at the public high school for the ninth grade, and she even had enough courage to audition for the school's show choir.

After an amazing four years that had its ups and downs, she blossomed into a beautiful flower! She discovered her latent love for musical theater, which in turn gave her a new confidence and belief in herself. Oddly enough, attending public high school also strengthened her faith. She found she had to take a stand for Christ instead of just blending in with all the other Christians at the Christian school. Needless to say, God knows what He is doing! He knows our child's entire life and what preparation she needs for her future. My daughter is now twenty-seven years old and lives several states away from home. I can now see how God used the move to public school to prepare her for attending a large university five hours from home and then taking her first job in Washington DC. She had developed a strong faith in God and a solid confidence in herself that transformed her into a wonderfully independent young woman ready to take on the world! We are both so glad we did not let fear keep us from obeying God! Learning to cultivate an ear to hear God's voice and a surrendered heart to obey it are keys to successfully navigate the different seasons of your child's life.

## SEASONS OF MATURITY

Character happens in the waiting. Some plants blossom and flower before others, but that doesn't make the slower-blooming flowers any less fragrant. I love to garden, but not all my vegetables are ready to be harvested at the same time. It seems like I wait forever for the first tomato, yet the green beans are ready in just weeks, but I've discovered the wait is so very worth it.

The field your child is striving to excel in will determine how long this season lasts. A young girl with aspirations to become an Olympic gymnast may reach her peak as a young teenager and not remain competitive in the sport after college. A child desiring to be a microbiologist won't be hitting his stride until well after college and graduate school. A world-class violin virtuoso likely remains in a constant season of maturing throughout an active career of playing concerts and teaching. Continually applying oneself, resisting distractions, and maintaining discipline and diligence during the years of developing one's gifts makes all the difference. Like the season of preparation, this season will take ongoing sacrifice and prioritizing between what is an important investment of time and effort and what is a waste of time.

> Whoever works his land will have plenty of bread,
> but he who follows worthless pursuits will have
> plenty of poverty.
> —PROVERBS 28:19

## SEASONS OF MULTIPLICATION

This is the one you wait for, the one where your child's hard work begins bearing fruit and he starts to see results. The young golfer whose countless hours on the driving range manifests into a flawless and automatic swing earning him a string of top-ten wins among a field of fierce competitors. The budding wordsmith whose love of words and reading has taken him from spelling bee champion to high school yearbook editor to award-winning collegiate journalist now enjoys a burgeoning career built upon the foundation of his love for words. Countless examples exist among those whose young lives demonstrate the adage that the harder we work, the luckier we seem to be.

Perhaps your child has a passion for evangelism or missions and actively participates in his youth group outreach activities. Imagine the thrill when the Lord begins to multiply the fruit of your child's fearless faithfulness by seeing his friends and, in turn, their friends come to know Christ. Now that is multiplication.

Francesca is in the season of multiplication as I write these words. She worked, practiced, studied, and honed her craft for years before anyone knew her name. Her ten-thousand hours are, for the most part, behind her, and she is now reaping the rewards of her diligence. She's been blessed to write and record two best-selling albums. She is enjoying her sixth hit radio single, has won five Gospel Music Association Dove Awards, and garnered a Grammy nomination. Countless fans have spoken and written thanking her for the impact her music has made on their lives. Her music is reaching a generation through the multiplied avenues of radio, television, movies, and live performance. Though it did not happen for her overnight, once multiplication took root, she can honestly say life indeed comes at you fast! Even her family is multiplying as she now also has a wonderful husband and a beautiful baby boy in addition to all the other blessings in her life.

## SEASONS OF DISAPPOINTMENT

But life for Franny wasn't always so rosy. Before the years where everything came together, she experienced ups and downs, disappointments, and failures just like everyone else. I could relate to you the countless meetings with "people of influence" whose promises to come alongside and help guide her career came to nothing. Or the countless press kits we mailed that got no response. She auditioned for TV, movie, and musical theater productions that she didn't get. Live performances, even the rare ones that actually paid something, ended up being canceled or turning out quite differently than we expected.

One notable occasion was when a local television station invited Franny to tape a live performance for broadcast at a later time. We showed up early at the place where the taping was to take place, and our jaws dropped. We were greeted by the producer and ushered to the back pool room of a smoky bar near the Orlando airport, where they were proud to announce it was twenty-five-cent beer night! In spite of having trouble hearing herself over the roar of rowdy bikers playing pool and drinking beer, she did a great job. We remember that night in particular and marvel to this day that the majority of those in the bar drinking beer and playing pool actually stopped playing to turn and listen intently as she played and sang about Jesus!

Franny also experienced deep, personal disappointments during those years. Some relationships didn't pan out as expected. Some people she thought were friends and had her best interests at heart ultimately let her down. Even moving to Nashville, though exciting, was a lonely and difficult experience at first. On the day she actually signed her record deal, she returned home to an empty house in a new city, hundreds of miles away from those who would have been the most eager to celebrate with her. The childhood dream of pursuing a career in dance was shattered when scoliosis progressed to the point of preventing her from going any further down that road. Each of us could just as easily list those times in our lives when we felt the sting of disappointment.

But during those times, faith kept us going. Franny had a dream and a strong belief in God's future for her life. Though disappointment reared its ugly head from time to time, she never let it destroy her dreams. God uses disappointment to build our character and teach us to persevere when things get rough, just as He did for Franny during those times in her life.

I have a dear friend who has been an amazing voice of wisdom and godliness in my life for almost twenty years. Together with her husband she has raised four amazing children. Her sobering thoughts will encourage you during the inevitable seasons of disappointment that will come:

> Sometimes what you've planned and intended doesn't pan out. It's easy to obsess over lost years and lost dreams. But the most frightening seasons in life can become the most treasured when we trust in the perfection and beauty of God's salvation through Christ and not in our own efforts to produce "good" children. God's Word, His mercy, grace, and peace restored my mind and renewed my devotion to serve Him after a season of brokenheartedness. I became focused on what Christ had done for me and not on what I had done for Him. In my opinion, the correct focus on Christ's work for us is the central key to raising children to love and serve God.
>
> In Christ, God absorbed my punishment! What a staggering gift. Children need a constant flow of mercy. They generally live fixated on themselves. They often love things that are not good for them.

They often listen to voices that lead them astray. They need to experience mercy when they've ruined something important.

Children need to understand that they won't naturally have what they need to accomplish God's plan for their lives. They will absolutely need God's help to do what He's called them to do. They will need His grace to achieve His will. And they need to see God as the author of all that they need. After all, whatever they do must be for His glory or it will be wasted, even if it looks very good to the rest of the world.

Children live in a world at war, both within themselves and outside of themselves. They need to be constantly assured that God is in control of all things, as He clearly tells us in His Word. We need to keep this precious and calming assurance constantly before them, that He is working all things pertaining to their lives out according to His own will, so that when things don't go as planned, they will not despair, nor become angry, but trust Him and rest in His great goodness.

## SEASONS OF HUMILITY

When Francesca took a semester off from school and went to Alabama to serve in an evangelism ministry school, she humbled herself and laid down her burgeoning music career before the Lord. At the time my husband confided to me he thought it probably was not the wisest thing to do from a "business" perspective, especially in light of the attention Franny had begun to receive for her music. In spite of his misgivings, we packed her up, kissed her good-bye, and prayed for God to meet her on this journey. Her experience, though a relatively short one, taught her a deep lesson about taking the lower place—in this case serving another ministry's vision, all the while sharing a small (very small) house with thirteen girls.

It is not uncommon for God to put us in situations where we are asked to help someone else make their dreams come true. For reasons not obvious to us at the time, and perhaps only for a season, God may require us to lay down our dreams, testing us in the process. Sometimes we will be given the opportunity to take the lower place to help someone else achieve their goals before being given the chance to achieve our own.

## SEASONS OF CHASTENING

*Chastening* is an old-fashioned word having to do with how God disciplines and instructs His children. It's not a popular word or concept in this modern age, but God still does it. He does it because He loves us and wants only the absolute best for His children. Whether this is a subject preached from the pulpit very frequently or not, God still chastens, and it's important to understand why. God calls us to hard obedience and to the narrow road. The road *is* narrow, and the Word says there are few who find it! At times we might be tempted to become prideful, especially if we have gifts or talents others do not. God will sometimes allow us to experience bitter disappointment, conviction, or even rebuke to remind us where our gifts come from in the first place. He'll discipline and correct us to help change our behavior and better conform us to His image. Chronological age brings no special immunity from God's gentle nudge or mid-course correction. His chastening has a point, and it's to bring us to repentance and to an understanding that God is sovereign in every area of our lives. The Bible says, "My son, do not despise the chastening of the LORD, nor be discouraged when you are rebuked by Him; for whom the LORD loves He chastens, and scourges every son whom He receives" (Heb. 12:5–6).

## SEASONS OF FAILURE

Life is a series of choices. Most of us have, at one time or another in our lives, made an improper choice and learned a difficult lesson the hard way. We may have made a wrong turn, taken the wrong road altogether, or made one bad choice that cost a scholarship or our place on the team. As adults, we are well aware that our actions have consequences. If you drive under the influence and get arrested for DUI, you can lose your license and your reputation—and it can go against your permanent record. If a teenage girl ends up pregnant, her dreams can be put on hold indefinitely and sometimes permanently. We learn from our poor choices about reaping and sowing and about the fruit of wrong decisions.

But this is not to say God can't redeem our mistakes. He certainly can, and does, and the Bible is chock-full of examples. The story of the prodigal son (Luke 15:11–32) illustrates the power of a father's love and the gift of redemption. The prodigal son came to a crossroad in life when he realized the error of his misspent youth and where his choices in life had led him. He chose to come home, and while he was still a long way off, his father ran to meet him, bringing gifts. When we've turned away from God's perfect will for our lives but recognize our sin and turn and repent, God always meets us where we are with open arms and a fresh start.

The road to excellence is often a hard and unforgiving one. Competition in this world doesn't seem to diminish but grows ever more demanding. There will always be someone willing to put in more hours than you, to work harder, and to take advantage of every opportunity to get a leg up.

It is especially important to encourage our children to buckle down and be diligent as they enter their teen years. These are years full of distraction, where peers and popularity place great demands on their time. Teenagers always find more fun in going to a friend's house to play video games or watch a movie than staying home to practice piano or get a head start on their research paper. A gentle reminder may be enough for some to stay focused and on course—our daughter was one. Others may need firmer boundaries and strong direction. In either case, being diligent will require setting priorities and establishing specific goals. Often it means giving up momentary pleasure for a future harvest—perhaps one of the most important disciplines we can instill early on with our children.

Failure can occur when we fail to persevere. Being disappointed is never fun, and the impulse to give up when not successful at first is a natural one. Thomas Edison performed more than a thousand experiments before he discovered electricity. Abraham Lincoln was elected president, but only after experiencing many of life's failures, including running for elected office and losing several times. But he persisted and was eventually elected to the highest office of the land and is today revered as one of the greatest presidents in American history.

Galatians 6:9 says it best: "And let us not grow weary while doing good, for in due season we shall reap if we do not lose heart." I remember an occasion when Franny was tested in the area of perseverance at an early age. She auditioned for the Orlando Ballet Company production of *The Nutcracker* when she was maybe eight years old. She was so excited to audition for the judges and was thoroughly convinced she would land a coveted role in the production as one of the "party children." About a week after the audition, letters were sent out informing the children whether they landed a spot in the production or not. Her letter arrived after what seemed like an eternity. I remember telling her the letter had arrived and asked her whether she wanted to pray before we opened it. She said yes, and I recall her saying no matter what the letter said, she would have a good attitude about it. Of course she agreed.

We hurriedly opened the letter, and to her utter disappointment she had been rejected. Oh, the tears and heartache that followed, I can't tell you! She was particularly upset with the judges who had rejected her! When she calmed down, we were able to help her accept the bitter news and to realize she wasn't being rejected as a person. She was very young at the time, and the ballet needed kids with a little more experience. When the next year finally rolled around, she auditioned again. This time when the letter arrived it contained better news, and she got to be one of the party children after all!

Franny didn't give up on dance because she was rejected on this occasion. She was disappointed but persevered, worked hard, and improved a lot during the next year.

It is important that we as parents encourage our children to persevere in their gifts. Franny was upset enough at the time of that first stinging disappointment to give up dance altogether, but she admitted, and we both knew, she loved dance too much to quit. Even at eight years old, children have sensitive egos, and they can be easily bruised. As parents we have to gently help them over life's inevitable disappointments and rejections to help keep them on their chosen paths. If, on the other hand, a child fails over and over again at something, it's probably time to pray and really press in to determine whether they are on the right path. We must guard against disappointment causing our kids to give up and abandon their dreams, especially if these are the dreams God has put in them.

Disappointment is a big part of life, and at times it's the very thing that sparks the determination needed to press in, press on, and succeed. If we have helped them set firm goals for their future, they will find a way to overcome disappointment and persevere past failure to meet those goals. The adage is still true: "If at first you don't succeed, try, try again!"

## SEASONS OF SUCCESS

As parents, this is what we wait for! Our child gets the acceptance letter and scholarship to the college of her choice. Or she makes the cheerleading squad. Or she gets the lead in the play. After trying out several times he makes the team. He finally gets on the honor roll. All their hard work now begins to pay off. Hopefully our children will enjoy lots of little successes over the years, each new success encouraging them to continue pressing in and pursuing their goal. Each success builds on the one before, setting up a pattern where it can be easier to clearly discern the path God has laid out for their lives. Confidence grows with each new milestone achieved. Success motivates. As adults, getting a raise or a promotion reminds us we are doing a good job. It's the same with our children.

## SEASONS OF ACCEPTANCE

Sometimes things happen to derail our hopes, dreams, and desires, and there is absolutely nothing we can do about it. How many times have we heard of a budding athlete who sustained a career-ending injury?

When my husband, Mike, was in high school playing football, he sustained a back injury that resulted in surgery, effectively ending any thought of playing football in college. He would likely tell you today, in spite of the lingering painful effects of his injury, it was probably the single most important influence that drove him to focus on music and ultimately lead him into a very successful career in the music world.

In Franny's case, scoliosis sabotaged her career in dance and her dreams of becoming a ballerina. But like the famous adage we've all heard, when God closes a door, He does, in fact, open a window. In Franny's case, her condition closed the door to dance but opened the music window in a huge way.

Both Franny and Mike had to accept their situations for what they were before they went on to be great in what God had actually called them to. You can do it, and you can encourage your children to do the same when circumstances are beyond their control.

## THE TIME IN BETWEEN

For all you moms reading this, you're well aware transition is the most difficult time of labor. Contractions are coming one on top of another, the pain is intense, you are feeling overwhelmed, and all you want to do is get off this train and go home! But the baby is right around the corner! Mike and I used to be certified instructors in the Bradley Method of Natural Childbirth, and I was blessed to coach many laboring women. I always reminded them during this difficult time that their baby would be in their arms soon. The prize they had waited nine months for was just about here. I would try to refocus their thinking off the pain and onto the prize! Transition was different for each of them, but it tended to last the longest for the ones who fought against it rather than relaxing and letting it happen.

In raising our children, each season will transition into the next. Some of those transitions will be seamless and painless. Some will be abrupt and come without warning. Others will require digging deep and trusting God with everything in you. God is faithful, so try to relax, and He will get you through!

## Bloom Where You're Planted

Sometimes your child is on the right path, but it may simply not be the right time. Learning to bloom where we're planted is a huge lesson we learned over the years. Franny served on the worship team at her church for several years while she was hoping to carve out a career in music. Some weeks she got a solo, but many weeks she didn't. She was content to simply be one of the voices on the team and serve in whatever way she was needed. To me, success and happiness is a matter of faithfully doing what God calls you to, however large or small the platform, and whether you are recognized in it or not.

At times it's important to simply let things marinate. If it feels like God has pushed the pause button on your child's dreams, it might be a time of testing to see if he will persevere and ultimately break through. God's economy is never wasteful. What your son or daughter has been faithful to and diligent in, God *will* redeem and ultimately use—perhaps in ways you could only have dreamed of years earlier. Try to relax, take a breath, and recognize the season your child is in before trying to leapfrog from one season to another.

## Questions to Think About

1. What season is my child currently in?

2. Is God using disappointment to build my child's character?

3. How can I help my child transition from one season to the next?

4. Am I encouraging my child to persevere even when things don't seem to be happening as fast as he'd like?

5. Is my child content to bloom where he's planted? Am I content to let him?

## PRAYER

*Father, You have made everything beautiful in its time. I'm grateful for the different seasons in my own life and my child's. Give me wisdom about what season my child is currently in, and help us to be diligent to mine every bit of goodness and wisdom from it we can. I don't want to rush my child into another season. Allow him to learn every lesson You have for him where he is right now. Give me the wisdom and discernment I need to help him through the inevitable times of transition. Thank You, Lord!*

# 14

# DON'T BE A HINDRANCE TO THE DREAM

T HERE ARE THINGS that can get in the way of our child's potential that we can't control. Some things we can and must if we are going to raise world changers. If we aren't careful, we can abort our child's dream and calling, often without knowing it. We may be able to dig deep and mine the gift. We may even be able to help our children recognize and acknowledge the door to God's path for their lives but fail in helping them unlock the door. There are several negative things parents unknowingly inflict on their kids to cause resentment and ultimately hinder the very things we are trying to accomplish.

## CRITICISM AND SARCASM

A soft answer turneth away wrath: but grievous words stir up anger.

—PROVERBS 15:1, KJV

Words carry more power than we realize. They can bring life or death to a child's dream. It's important to be careful with the words we speak, and we should always endeavor to edify, exhort, and encourage our kids in all they do. Constantly nagging our kids (or our spouses for that matter) does not produce good fruit. We want to be encouragers—the ones our kids can come to when life, friends, and pressures at school get to be too much.

Growing up, I was exposed to lots of criticism, and, unfortunately, it had the effect of turning me away from my parents. I was afraid to ask their advice, especially during the young teen years when I needed it most. I knew engaging my parents would ultimately end in criticism. As the middle child I was already feeling vulnerable and somewhat passed over, so my ego was pretty fragile. I felt if I revealed my inner feelings, there was a good chance I would be ridiculed. So I did what lots of teens do. I turned to friends and ultimately got involved with a boyfriend way too young. I sought encouragement from all the wrong places and found it where I could.

No parent intentionally sets out to be a source of criticism or put-down in their child's life, but all too often we are. If you have multiple children living at home, this is an area needing careful attention. What are we modeling to the others when we take a critical swipe or lob a sarcastic put-down at one of the children? Do siblings relate well to one another and build each other up, or are they quick to attack their brothers and sisters with relentless teasing and criticism? It's up to us to decide what we will tolerate in our families.

It's a parent's responsibility to correct their children and to set the proper tone in the home. We must be vigilant and observant and willing to guide them and correct our kids when they do or say something wrong or hurtful, including using words as weapons. A parent's correction is always best done in love and with discernment. It is possible to criticize constructively if we remain clear in our message, keeping it positive, and providing we're not reacting out of emotion in the moment. There is a difference in correcting a child's behavior and criticizing who they are as a person. As much as you're able, do it in a calm and loving manner and do it privately, without other siblings or friends present. The main thing is to endeavor not to devalue the child but correct the behavior.

Also, we need to be careful not to label or brand our children. Repeatedly telling a child he is lazy, stupid, or mean only makes him believe those things about himself. Children believe what parents say about them, and if you tell them they will never amount to anything, you are practically guaranteeing they won't.

Sarcasm is another sharp-edged no-no. Anyone who knows me knows I tend to have a somewhat sarcastic sense of humor. My personality type (phlegmatic) loves to tease, and I delight (in love of course!) to see people squirm. I can be funny when I'm on a roll, but it is usually at someone else's expense. As a result, I've had to learn to curb my impulse. I came to realize early on that my daughter would not respond particularly well to sarcasm. She is a "words of affirmation" girl, and I am not. I think because I grew up in a critical home, I tend to have difficulty believing something nice said about me. I'm much more of an "acts of service" person. If you do something *for* me, it means a lot more than if you say something nice *about* me. But my daughter isn't like that, and I learned when she was still a little girl I would get a better response from her if I affirmed her often and told her she was doing a great job. Be careful, however, not to fall into the trap of overusing positive words to the point of rendering them meaningless when most needed.

Sarcasm by its very nature is both biting and critical. The dictionary defines it this way: "a sharp and often satirical or ironic utterance designed to cut or give pain," which doesn't sound like something belonging in our parenting arsenal, does it? Young children typically don't understand it, are simply confused by it, and think mom is plain weird if sarcasm is used in place of simple, honest communication. Older children typically *do* understand sarcasm, but it can be just as damaging as criticism. In fact, sarcasm actually *is* criticism in a backhanded kind of way. Saying sarcastically "Great job, Einstein" to a child who didn't do well on a school project or quiz cuts deeply and can leave a lasting mark.

Luke 6:45 says it best: "A good man out of the good treasure of his heart brings forth good; and an evil man out of the evil treasure of his heart brings forth evil. For out of the abundance of the heart his mouth speaks."

Sarcasm is part of the everyday world around us, but it is not a useful or uplifting element of parenting. Instead of building up and edifying, sarcasm leaves its target feeling belittled. I want the abundance of my heart to be uplifting to others and not cutting and condemning. Jesus reminds us, "And just as you want men to do to you, you also do to them likewise" (Luke 6:31).

## LOW EXPECTATIONS

We see the fruit all around us of parents whose expectations for their children were set too low. These are parents who failed to provide strong direction and guidance while their children were young and are now enabling their young adults to drift.

Criticism and sarcasm may originate, in some misguided way, from a desire to see your child achieve something. Knowing a child is not living up to their potential and not understanding how to motivate him might cause a desperate parent to resort to criticism in an attempt at reverse psychology. The attempt is usually made out of frustration and a lack of understanding of the child's needs. On the other hand, setting expectations too low diminishes their desire to actually accomplish much of anything in life. Some parents never learned how to dream for their own lives or perhaps had their dreams dashed somewhere along the way. As a result, dreaming big for their children, setting positive expectations, and moving mountains to help their children achieve their goals is something that doesn't come naturally to them. It would be those parents I am particularly eager to impact by this book. It is *not* too late to begin right now today!

Some parents don't know where to begin to motivate their child. Some fear their child will ultimately fail to accomplish her goals, so they avoid the possibility altogether by never getting started. Some are afraid their child will grow up, become independent, and leave home. Believe me, I recognize *that* fear all too well. I wish more than anything my daughter lived nearby and I could see her every day. But I know full well she couldn't begin to live out her destiny living at home with mom and dad. We can take joy in equipping and launching our children into adulthood by setting the stage, pointing the way in love with every expectation for success and happiness.

## THE LAND OF GOOD ENOUGH

My husband has always joked that the world seems to be run by C students. Just go shopping and you'll know what he means. Observe the young woman ringing up your purchase who's not able to make correct change; the young man bagging your groceries who puts the hot rotisserie chicken in with the ice cream; the waiter who continually forgets to bring you the side of ranch dressing. These are the kids who are running our world. They seem to live in the land of "good enough." It seems the average employee works just hard enough not to get fired, and their employers pay them just enough so they won't quit. These are kids who did just well enough in school not to flunk out, and as long as they can live at home, eat mom's cooking, have the newest iPhone, and hang out with friends, life is good enough. Sometimes I just want to scream, "Where did these people come from?"

Though there seems to be an epidemic of "good enough" all around us, it doesn't have to be the path your children take. Yes, hard work, determination, sacrifices, and effort on your part and the part of your children is required, but compare the dividends. No one brings their baby home from the hospital hoping they'll grow up with the career aspiration to stock shelves at the local convenience store. We all want more for our kids, but more doesn't happen by accident. Raised by different parents, Francesca might have had a very different life. There is nothing extraordinary about her other than the fact we recognized the gifts and talents in her at a young age and worked purposefully and intentionally to bring them to fullness in her life. We worked hard and she worked hard. "Good enough" was neither in our vocabulary nor in hers. We didn't want her floating aimlessly through life because we possessed a firm belief in purpose and destiny. We know far too many young people who are not living up to their potential, and it saddens me to see it. To be honest, this very thing was perhaps my greatest motivation in writing *Growing Great Kids*.

## NO GOAL SETTING

If we don't know where we are going, how will we know when we get there? Learning to set goals gives you something to measure and the time line to measure it against. Goals motivate and help keep you focused on what's important. When I was a young twenty-something and just beginning to think maybe my life did have a purpose, I began setting goals. I wrote out several goals I was eager to achieve in the next year and put them in a pretty little box. I closed the lid, and truthfully I forgot I had even written them down. Several months later I found the box and reread my goals and was astounded to find that I'd accomplished every single one of them! Right then and there I realized the power of setting goals and writing them down.

In the act itself we set ourselves up to succeed when we write down our goals. I've since learned there really *is* something to goal setting. We became students of the process, and Mike and I taught what we knew about setting measurable goals to Franny. Goals are great motivators! If your child doesn't learn to set and work to achieve goals, it's as if he's adrift in the ocean without a paddle. Just like us, if he doesn't know where he's headed, how will he know when he gets there?

## No Standard of Excellence

If it's true the world is run by C students, then the fault lies with the parents. It can be difficult to motivate an unmotivated kid and harder still to deal with their grumbling and complaining. But God calls us to pursue excellence in character and in deed. Ecclesiastes 9:10 reads, "Whatever your hand finds to do, do it with all your might."

We are motivated to pursue excellence because excellence honors God as well as the trust He's placed in us by giving us those gifts. We are to pursue excellence but *not* perfection. As Franny wrote in her song "Free to Be Me," "perfection is my enemy." We can drive our kids crazy and do real harm by demanding perfection from them, but we hold them back if we don't require excellence in all they do. Excellence is simply going beyond what's expected, rising above the standard, and leaving things better than we found them. To pursue excellence is to pursue being the best we can possibly be with the gifts and talents God has given us, with humility and the understanding we aren't in competition with others, and the blessing of doing it for God's glory.

To excel is to simply do the best *we* can do to honor God with our lives.

I love the way 1 Corinthians 15:58 is stated in the Amplified Bible: "Therefore, my beloved brethren, be firm (steadfast), immovable, always abounding in the work of the Lord [always being superior, excelling, doing more than enough in the service of the Lord], knowing and being continually aware that your labor in the Lord is not futile [it is never wasted or to no purpose]."

If something is worth doing, it is certainly worth doing well, allowing it to flow from and return to our relationship with God. If we truly are teaching our children to "love the Lord God with all your heart, with all your soul and with all your mind" (Matt. 23:37), then as they grow in their understanding of what this means, our children will realize excellence is a simple matter of the heart. What we do flows from who we are.

## THE AMERICAN IDOL SYNDROME

If you've ever watched *American Idol*, you've surely seen the audition episodes where they showcase some of the really awful singers. I find these episodes terribly sad because these singers, and very likely their parents, are completely deceived about their talents and abilities. Too many of them really believe they can sing when it's painfully obvious to the world they have no musical ability.

Some of these parents are simply bound and determined their children deserve to be the next *American Idol*, regardless of whether they're gifted musically or not. After the judges lower the boom and tell them the truth, it's interesting to see the anger and tears that well up. How dare these judges say something unkind about their baby! It's so sad to me that they either have no idea or choose to remain clueless about their child's musical giftings.

What good could it possibly do for parents to encourage their child to believe in an impossible dream or believe a lie about herself? Wouldn't it be wiser to seek an honest appraisal of your child's gifts when she's young and find out what she really *is* gifted in? In failing to do this, these *American Idol* parents set their son or daughter up for massive public embarrassment and failure and, in many cases, years wasted going in the wrong direction. My best advice is to look for independent verification of your child's ability. Talk to a music teacher or coach or mentor early on if you believe they have promise in a specific area.

As parents, we tend to be biased about our kids. Every little thing they accomplish proves to us they are exceptionally gifted. Sometimes it's true—but often it's not. To prove my point, pick your favorite song and look for some of the videotaped renditions of it on YouTube. See how many people try to sing, play, or dance to their favorite tune. I am amazed how many of them take place in churches with young girls singing poorly to accompaniment tracks. I'm all about encouraging young people to follow their passion and pursue what's in their hearts, but a dose of private reality can save a lot of public heartache later on.

I think some parents want their child to excel at something more than their child does. I understand it reflects well on us as parents when our kids do well or accomplish something. It simply does, and there is nothing wrong with that. The danger is in allowing that to become the motivating factor. As we diligently seek God about our child's gifts and talents (or lack thereof), He will reveal their path. Most kids won't end up on stage as the American Idol. Is that OK with you? If it's not, you may have some serious soul searching to do.

The majority of people won't live their lives in the limelight or as a sports star or a famous actor. I want to help you dig deep and find that special gift in your child that will change the world the way God determined. An "ordinary" gift can be extraordinary when executed with passion and purpose. If you've ever had a fabulous teacher, then you know just what I mean. The teacher who took your boring history class and made it come alive and turned your least favorite class into your most favorite. Or the plumber/electrician/landscaper who did such a fantastic job at your home. Or the chef who labors obscurely in the kitchen of your favorite restaurant and doesn't have a TV show yet produces the most delicious meals.

What I'm trying to convey is, be realistic in your expectations for your child. There is more than one thing they excel at, even if it's not an occupation that brings the glare of the spotlight. Be mindful how you measure greatness. It doesn't usually come with fame or fortune but in a great reputation of excellence, honesty, work ethic, and integrity. Let your goal for your child be to do her work as unto the Lord with excellence, and He will raise her up to the level He desires. Most of us are called to excellence in obscurity.

## INDIFFERENCE

Some parents just don't care. If you've read this far, this likely doesn't apply to you! But we all know parents of good kids who just seem indifferent to their children's needs. They are parents who are uninvolved in their children's lives and unsupportive of their dreams. Some parents may be in a financial or emotional crisis and don't know how to cope. Sometimes it's the result of a painful divorce. Or some may be battling depression or anxiety. Or some may be working so much they don't have time to be involved in their child's life. Still others may leave it up to the school or church to do the work for them. Children are a gift. Psalm 127:3 teaches, "Behold, children are a heritage from the

LORD. The fruit of the womb is a reward." Parenting is not a casual occupation. God gave you your children as a reward, and we honor God by caring for and loving our children. Matthew 18:5 says, "Whoever receives one little child like this in My name receives Me." Serving and loving our children is what allows us to experience Christ more fully. He teaches us humility and the precious gift of serving others.

## WORKAHOLIC PARENTS

It's easy to get our priorities mixed up. Some of us think if we give our children every toy and gizmo under the sun, they will know how much we love them. We work hard to provide a big home, expensive cars, designer clothes, and the newest gadget. What some of us fail to realize is the time we spend with our children is far more valuable in their eyes, and in the eyes of God, than anything we can give them. In our misguided effort to provide for our children, we can be denying them the most valuable thing they need—our time and attention. Too many families have bought into the insidious lie of more is better perpetuated in our culture—a bigger home, nicer car, more expensive vacation, the biggest television, and the most expensive toys.

Mike and I have been unabashed proponents of home-based businesses for American families for this very reason: they provide the opportunity for at least one parent to stay at home and raise their families and their income at the same time.

There is an entire generation of latchkey kids whose working parents are not very involved in their lives. In the years to come, your son and daughter won't remember what you gave them, but they will recall the time you spent with them. Many families need both parents to work simply to make ends meet. Others are single-parent households, and being as available as we want to be may not be possible. But to a large extent, our culture is defined by Madison Avenue, and when we see all the cool stuff available, we want it, both for our kids and for ourselves! I believe it's critically important to rethink our priorities and take a look at how involved we are in our children's lives. Maybe it's possible to do without that second car. Is there a way to adjust your lifestyle to create more family time?

One vital family tradition that seems to be rapidly dying away is the family dinner. Mealtimes are a great time to communicate as a family, talking and sharing what happened during the day. Make it a "cell-phone free zone" for an uninterrupted time of conversation and family bonding. Or consider a family night where you do something fun like order pizza and play a family game. Even though there were only three of us in our family, we loved having game night. We played endless games of Yahtzee, Uno, Life, Monopoly, Scrabble, and Clue. Franny always loved those nights, and we learned playing games just how competitive she was! She loved to win! (She takes after her dad a lot!)

Consider undertaking a family project, maybe tackling a big job around the house or going down to volunteer as a family at the local hospital or homeless shelter. Take a bike ride together or go for a hike. Make s'mores. There are loads of things families can do that don't cost a thing. We all tend to spend time on the things most important to us. Time spent with your children will be remembered and treasured long after the gadget of the month has disappeared.

## QUESTIONS TO THINK ABOUT

1. Am I using criticism to try to motivate my child?

2. What are some ways I can constructively criticize my child without condemning her?

3. Am I overly sarcastic?

4. Are my expectations for my child high or low?

5. Am I helping my child set goals?

6. Do I require my children to strive for excellence in all they do?

7. Am I or my spouse a workaholic? How can we change that?

8. Do we have a regular family night? If not, how can we change that?

## PRAYER

*Heavenly Father, above all, I want to be a bridge to my child's dreams, not a hindrance. Help me to see if there is anything in my parenting that might be hindering my child. Help me to put a guard on my tongue and only speak words that will correct and edify, build up, and strengthen my child. Help me to have the right expectations for my child, no more or less than You have for her. Give me guidance as I teach my child to set goals and strive for excellence in whatever she puts her hand to. Forgive me for thinking things are more important than time. Show me ways my family and I can spend quality time together and make memories lasting a lifetime!*

# 15

# COMMON PARENTING TRAPS

T HE ENEMY SETS lots of traps for parents. The last thing he wants us to do is raise world changers who live with power and anointing on their lives. He will do all he can to throw roadblocks and snares in our way. Some are subtle and some are obvious, but they all have one purpose: to knock our children off the path God appointed for them.

## FAVORITISM AND JEALOUSY

I raised an only child, so I didn't have to deal much with the issue of favoritism. Unfortunately, however, it's prevalent in many families. Jealousy and favoritism are also big themes in the Old Testament and important issues to understand. When we read the stories of the patriarchs, the destructive effects and devastating consequences of favoritism and jealousy are evident. Genesis 21:9–10 tells of Sarah's intense jealousy of Hagar and ultimately of Hagar's son, Ishmael. Isaac favored Esau and Rebekah favored Jacob. Jacob favored Joseph, and in each case, serious conflict arose. From Abraham to Jacob, conflicts continued in the family line, which led to wars and fostered prejudices and cultural hatred still in existence today.

Whatever our feelings about our individual children, it is vital to show love equally to each one and discipline them fairly and with justice. It wouldn't be judged a sin to prefer one child over another, but it is vitally important not to express that preference in an obvious way. Five children from the same mother and father are likely to exhibit vastly different behavioral characteristics, personality traits, and physical attributes. It would be only natural for one of those five to possess characteristics more pleasing or more like mom or dad, causing the one to be preferred over the others. Or a mom with four boys finally welcoming a precious daughter to the mix might have a love for her different than for the boys, but she must take care not to express her love in a way that could lead to conflict and jealousy.

The snare of jealousy is what caused Cain to murder Abel. Proverbs 14:30 says, "A sound heart is life to the body, but envy is rottenness to the bones." And Proverbs 27:4 states, "Wrath is cruel and anger a torrent, but who is able to stand before jealousy?"

Scripture warns that jealousy is worse than wrath or anger! It is a destructive force within families, and parents must be vigilant and not allow jealousy to take root and grow between siblings or parents. As believers, we want our homes to be places of peace and safety for our families, and to model Christian love at all times. Too often in movies and television, the modern family is depicted as selfish and dysfunctional, with siblings constantly teasing, fighting, and at each other's throats. To be a light in a dark world by modeling what a healthy loving family looks like is just one collateral benefit of raising kids who love, respect, and uplift their brothers and sisters.

## Unfulfilled Dreams

It's not uncommon for parents to impose unfulfilled dreams on their children. We recognized this trap early on raising our daughter. I determined Franny would never be a "mini-me." She naturally gravitated to and landed in the performing arts but plowed new ground quite apart from our experience. It would have been easy for me to fall into the common trap of pushing her to fulfill the dreams and goals I came close to achieving but that remained just out of reach. Our goal was to provide the proper environment and the tools and the encouragement to let *her* gifts rise to the surface.

Following in our parents' footsteps, or carrying on the family business, is a great tradition. Just look at how family names have described those family's trades and professions—names like Miller, Cooper, Baker, and Smith. Well, you get the picture! The danger arises when parents push children in a specific direction to fulfill their own unrealized dreams. If dad got close to realizing a professional sports career but never quite made it, he may be bound and determined his son will follow in his footsteps, regardless of the son's interest in or talent for sports. Or in families where celebrated lawyers go back for generations in the proud family tree, there can be incredible pressure on a child to follow the same familiar path, in spite of any interest in or aptitude for the law. Some families blatantly, or inadvertently, drive their children to make specific college or university choices for similar reasons. We can agree that any child who desires to please mother or father can easily be maneuvered to make a parent-pleasing decision with their future. But what God-ordained destinies do we risk knocking off course or subverting altogether in the process?

Gifts and passions are often passed on in a family, but sometimes new gifts will erupt without warning, springing up for the first time in a family's lineage. In Mike's family, there wasn't any extraordinary musical talent he is aware of going back several generations. Yet he was given an enormous musical gift and was able to explore and exploit his gifts completely in his career. His parents didn't dissuade him or try to mold him into something he wasn't destined to be. They recognized his gifts early on, made sacrifices so he could fully explore them, and encouraged and supported him along the way.

Let's purpose to find out who our kids are and what's unique about them, call out their gifts, support their goals and dreams, and see what God does from there. We can't expect our kids will be just like us. They won't be! My daughter is gifted musically, as I was, but our personalities and expression of our gifts are like night and day!

## CHILD OR IDOL?

In the spirit of full disclosure, this is the area where Mike and I nearly slipped off the cliff and failed for a season. God graciously pointed it out to us, and when we realized our error, we quickly repented. We all love our children so much, and though we say we completely entrust them to God, we sometimes really don't. We worry, we fret, and we stress—not exactly the fruit of the Spirit! Any child can become an idol to his parents, and unless we're careful, we risk upsetting the balance God designed for healthy family life. This can be particularly true if you have an extremely gifted child or an only child, and we had both in one! This can also be true for parents with a child who is handicapped or very ill or has special needs. Any child can easily become their parents' complete focus and receive all their time, attention, and resources. When that happens, we run the risk of centering our lives on our children to the exclusion of our spouse.

More parents are choosing to have only one child, and more

women are waiting until their thirties to have children, creating smaller only-child families by default. According to the US Census Bureau there are about sixteen million only-children, representing about 20 percent of all children in America today, up from only 10 percent fifty years ago.[1] With the recent economic downturn, more and more parents are opting for just one child for purely economic reasons.

Mike and I were blessed with one child, and a terrific one at that, but not by choice. If it had been our choice, we would have filled the house with kids! But God, who knows the end from the beginning, in His wisdom made us an only-child family. When Franny was one and a half, I suffered an ectopic, or tubal, pregnancy that caused enough internal damage to prevent us from having more children. I had laparoscopic surgery in an attempt to correct it, but the damage was done. We tried adoption, hiring attorneys and completing our home study, a detailed, written report of your family written by a social worker to see if you are qualified to adopt, but every time we got close, things fell apart and the adoption fell through. It took awhile for me to accept we would only have one child, but eventually, with the Lord's help, we accepted it and moved forward.

## THE THREE MUSKETEERS

Matthew 10:37 powerfully teaches, "He who loves father or mother more than Me is not worthy of Me. And he who loves son or daughter more than Me is not worthy of Me."

When I really saw and embraced this scripture for the first time, I was deeply convicted. For Jesus to say we are not worthy of Him got my attention. More than anything, I want to live a life worthy of my Savior and to honor Him in everything I do. I don't want anything to come between Him and me. We had to let God unveil this truth to us in His perfect timing. God gently revealed this to Mike and me when Franny first moved away. We had wrapped our lives up in hers for so long that we were in danger of making her an idol. When He pointed this scripture out to us, we repented for loving her more than loving Christ. It was time for us to fully trust God with her life and her future. It was time to let her go. But it was hard! Our lives and her life had been intertwined together for a long time. We used to quote Ecclesiastes 4:12 all the time, "A threefold cord is not quickly broken." We were the three musketeers! Her dreams had become our dreams, and it was hard to tell where she ended and we began.

When Franny moved away, we simply had to find the life God had for us. The season of being the main force and primary influence in our daughter's life was over. It was good for her *and* for us to accept this new season as it unfolded.

It can be tempting to want to hold on to our kids forever, but the inevitable day comes when we have to let them go and allow them to find the life they are born to live. If you are the parent of young children, this seems hard to imagine right now, but it is important to realize there will come a day when your kids will be gone and your house will be empty. Let me assure you, there *is* life after parenting! We simply enter an exciting new phase. I recommend maintaining your own interests and activities as much as possible, so when the time comes for your kids to leave home and be launched into their futures, you aren't left with empty hands and an empty heart. Be proactive in keeping your marriage first and foremost in your family. Remember, God gave your spouse to you first, then your children. Keep the flame burning bright now, go on dates, and remember why you got married in the first place. Then, when the kids are grown and gone, you won't be left simply staring at each other and wondering what to talk about!

How do you identify yourself? For a long time I was "Franny's mom." My identity was wrapped up in hers. The way we identify ourselves can sometimes reveal what holds us captive. I only want to be a bondslave to one master, and that's Jesus! I'm more than Franny's mom (although I'm proud to be), and now I'm in a new season of life where I can even call myself a writer. I never saw *that* coming, but God has wonderfully creative ways of wooing us down new paths!

## Selfishness

We live in a world where self is king. We are self-absorbed and self-seeking, and we think, "It's all about me!" Rather than seeking His purpose for our lives, our focus turns inward and says, "What about ME?" Much to my shame, I've discovered there is a deep root of selfishness in me. But by God's grace and continued conviction He has been able to pull it out of me. I grew up in a family where self was the dominating force, so selfishness naturally followed.

How do you know if selfishness is taking root? Here are a few questions to ask yourself:

1. Are you insensitive to the needs of your children?

2. Do you get angry when things don't go your way?

3. Do you feel like you deserve more than you have?

4. Are you arrogant and opinionated? Do you insist on having your way?

5. Do you talk about yourself more than you talk about others?

6. Are you lazy and sloppy?

7. Are you stingy?

8. Do you love to be the center of attention?

9. Are you financially irresponsible?

10. Are you pursuing your own goals at the expense of your children?

I can still answer yes to a couple of those questions, but I'm a work in progress. The Lord has taught many lessons in humility, and although it doesn't come naturally to me, I find I am less selfish and more others-oriented than I used to be. I still don't like it when things don't go my way, but I find that the closer I walk with the Lord, the more quickly I respond to His nudges and I am able to repent promptly.

I believe we should live a life of daily self-examination and repentance. In 1 Corinthians 15:31 Paul said, "I die daily," and we need to as well. The best advice I can give to avoid the trap of selfishness is to stay in the Word, pray without ceasing, and look for opportunities to serve. Volunteer for a homeless shelter or a food pantry. When you see how many people live without even the basic necessities, it will help to enlarge your perspective and cure your selfishness.

One gentle reminder—you will have your children for a very short time. Treasure the years and the day-in day-out routines. Put aside the cell phone and all those nameless distractions, and focus on the little one right in front of you. Let them know they are more important to you than the newest app or Twitter comment. The years will fly by, and the opportunities to love them and serve them, nurture and support them will vanish like frost under a hot sun. Cherish the moments, love hard, and be ruthless in rooting out selfishness in your life.

## UNREALISTIC EXPECTATIONS

We must be careful of the demands we place on our children. It's reasonable to expect a standard of excellence, but it is also easy to go overboard. We can overschedule and overtax a young child pretty quickly. In our desire to help a child to get into a great college, we might overschedule too many extracurricular activities for them, and after a season, they are burned out. Or we might really want our son to play basketball, but unlike dad who is 6 feet 3 inches, our boy is only 5 feet 4 inches. Or we might expect our child who is an average student to win a scholarship to a top Ivy League school when their SAT scores don't measure up.

My friend Sally sums it up well:

> We were realistic with our kids. As much as our son might have liked hearing us say that he could one day play for the NFL if he really wanted to, the fact was no, he couldn't! We supported their interests and required them to follow through on commitments they made, but we were more concerned with how it would shape their character than influence their abilities. Too often it's the parents who force the dream. We saw that played out again and again through the high school years, as parents would project their passion onto their children, especially in the area of athletics. We were our kid's biggest fans, but it had nothing to do with their performance.

We need to have realistic expectations. If we've pressed in and heard God's heart on the matter, we won't run the risk of projecting unrealistic expectations on our kids. We must learn to accept our children's limitations and love and accept them the way God made them. When we pray, listen to God, and listen to our children, we can avoid this trap.

## NEGATIVE PEOPLE AND RELATIVES AND DREAM THIEVES

Don't we all have at least one friend or relative who questions absolutely everything we do? We plug away at raising great kids only to have those negative words inject doubt and derail our confidence. We begin to question our parenting abilities and the dreams we have for our children because of one insensitive remark. People will sometimes say things without ever considering the consequences or thinking about how they sound. Some simply believe they know better than us when it comes to raising our children, and they are not shy about letting us know what they think.

Sometimes it's a mother-in-law, or it might be a friend, coworker, or sibling. I didn't share everything God showed me about my daughter with everyone I talked to. Some dreams are just for you and God. I didn't even always tell Franny all the things her dad and I prayed for her. She didn't need to know. We still pray for Franny every day, but she needs to live her life and hear God for herself, her husband, and son.

Some of us share too much! God has taught me to take care whom I share my dreams with, and I've learned the hard way to obey Him. There are many who will try to steal your dreams. Either they were never able to dream for themselves, or they're jealous or just plain ornery—it doesn't really matter. But try to use discernment before sharing every little detail about what God has shown you for your family. Continue to earnestly seek God for your child, and let Him share His dreams with you.

# CHILD-CENTERED HOMES

In many homes, the inmates seem to be running the asylum! Many parents don't enjoy their kids because, honestly, they're brats. You see them running around or screaming in restaurants while you're trying to have a quiet meal. At the grocery store they are wailing because they don't get what they want. They throw a fit at the dinner table because the parents served a food they don't like. Are you kidding me? Since when does the child rule the roost? What are those parents thinking? We put up way too much with willful disobedience, rebellion, stubbornness, and foolish behavior.

Are you your child's best friend, or are you, as my pastor likes to put it, a "benevolent dictator"? We are called to steward our families and to love and discipline our children. Have you ever been in a home where the parents don't set any boundaries? The children do as they please, say as they please, and demand attention constantly. They terrorize their parents and everyone around them. Parents are inconsistent with them and don't apply godly, biblical discipline. They try the 1-2-3 method with dismal results.

We have no problem following the Lord in so many areas, yet when it comes to raising children, we listen to the world's advice rather than the Word of God, which warns us in Proverbs 13:24, "He who spares his rod hates his son, but he who loves him disciplines him promptly." Another word for promptly is early. If they learn to obey you at two, you'll have fewer problems when they hit sixteen!

One time when Franny was around four years old, she got very mad at me because I was asking her to do something she didn't want to do. She looked right at me with a scowl on her face and said, "I don't like you!" She threw the gauntlet down, and right then and there I knew I had a decision to make. Either

I was going to be her friend or I was going to be her parent. I chose parent. I said calmly, "You don't have to like me, but you do have to obey me." She started to cry, so I hugged her. She said, "Mommy, I love you, and I'm sorry!" Of course I forgave her and told her I loved her too. But she knew from then on, I meant what I said and she was not running the house!

Our children need to learn early on that instant obedience is expected and failure to obey has serious consequences. If your child can't obey you, how will he ever be able to obey God? And if he isn't able to obey in the small things, how will he obey when his life is in danger? It's critical to set boundaries with children. It gives them a sense of security and shows them that their parents care. In fact, children want boundaries and function much better and feel safer with them. As long as you communicate clearly what you want them to do and stay consistent, you'll get results. Remember, each of us is born with a sin nature. And the Word says in Proverbs 22:15 says, "Foolishness is bound up in the heart of a child; the rod of correction will drive it far from him." I often wonder about the epidemic of attention deficit disorder prevalent among children today. When I was growing up, childish behavior was just kids being kids, and it needed to be trained out of them. I'm fully aware that ADHD or ADD is a real diagnosis for some children, but sometimes I wonder if it's ADD or, in some cases, AD-DEMON!

## WHICH CAME FIRST— MARRIAGE OR CHILD?

Before your child was a twinkle in your eye, your spouse was there for you. After junior is long gone, your spouse will still be there for you. We forget our children are going to grow up, leave home, and be launched into the life God calls them to. Child rearing is only a part of our lives. If we make children the priority rather than our spouses, what happens when the children leave? Where does that leave the marriage?

Here are more words of wisdom from my friend Robert about the importance of putting your marriage first:

> I have seen throughout the years a pitfall that a lot of married couples walk into blindly. We easily miss the instruction to help us avoid this. I've heard men and women alike say, "There is nothing that would come between me and my children." In reality, a more accurate statement would be, "I would never allow anything to come between me and my wife (or me and my husband), not even my children." This may seem odd and go against what a lot of parents instinctively believe. But I believe Scripture teaches us that the husband-wife relationship is the most important relationship humans can have! It is the first human relationship ever recorded in the Bible. It was so important to the Lord. He stated that He hates divorce. Think about it; He hates divorce.
>
> A man is not commanded to love his children as Christ loved the church and gave Himself for it, but rather to love his wife as Christ loved the church and gave Himself for it. In other words, as men, our wives are absolutely the most important relationship we have!
>
> It is true the Lord refers to loving us as His children, but when it comes to our relationship with our Savior and our future with Him, He refers to us as His bride. This is not an accident, and I truly believe it shows us how important the Lord views the marriage relationship. This is the platform on which we build our families and teach our children how to be

future husbands, wives, fathers, and mothers. It is from the firm foundation of a strong husband-wife relationship we are able to teach our children how to be all the things we desire for them from the time they are born! The real trap is we allow the children to become the center point of the family and then begin to neglect the marriage. In the family, the husband and wife are the most important relationship!

## LAST WORDS

I'm so proud of you for taking the time to read this far. You've just made an important investment in your child and your parenting. I'm looking forward to hearing your stories and how you are applying these principles in your family. I can't wait to learn about what you're doing to bring out all the treasure living in your child. You are an intentional parent, moving forward with faith and expectation. Here's my prayer for you:

*Father, thank You for touching these beautiful mothers (and grandmothers) and devoted fathers (and grandfathers) with Your truths. Walk closely with each of them as they raise their children to love You and honor You with their lives. Inspire them to dig deep and guide their children to uncover every gift, talent, and purpose You deposited in them before the foundation of the world. Day by day, encourage them to follow Your lead in all they do, and teach them to lead by setting an example of humility, diligence, integrity, and excellence.*

*Holy Spirit, draw close to each heart and strengthen them when difficulties and challenges arise. Give them wisdom every day and the patience to keep moving forward no matter what. Clearly show them all the world-changing potential in their precious child. Direct them, guide them, and stay close to them every day. In Jesus's mighty name, amen.*

There is extraordinary music yet to be composed and incredible world records waiting to be broken. Life-saving cures are still to be discovered, and life-changing technologies need to be invented. Transforming books are longing to be written, and startling paintings are ready for the artist's touch. Millions of people are waiting and needing to have the gospel revealed to them. Your child was born with the bright flame of possibility and promise. There are beautiful jewels and veins of gold deep inside your little one. All the ingredients for greatness are there in your child. Yes, yours. You'll need to be willing to dream big, work hard, pray consistently, speak life, and have faith. It only takes the faith of a mustard seed to move mountains and change lives. And that faith, more than anything else, grows great kids!

# NOTES

## Chapter 1—Gifts and Callings

1. Dictionary.com, s.v. "mine," http://dictionary.reference.com/browse/mine (accessed July 27, 2011).
2. Jack Hayford, general ed., *Spirit-Filled Life Bible* (Nashville: Thomas Nelson, Inc., 1991), emphasis added.
3. "Free to be Me" by Francesca Battistelli, copyright © 2008 by Word Music, LLC. All rights reserved. Used by permission.
4. "Jesus Loves Me" by Anna B. Warner. Public domain.
5. Malcolm Gladwell, *Outliers* (New York: Hachette Book Group, Inc., 2008).

## Chapter 2—The Power of a Parent's Words

1. Beliefnet.com, "Lady Bird Johnson," http://www.beliefnet.com/Quotes/Inspiration/L/Lady-Bird-Johnson/Children-Are-Likely-To-Live-Up-To-What-You-Believe.aspx (accessed September 16, 2011).
2. Biblesoft's *New Exhaustive Strong's Numbers and Concordance With Expanded Greek-Hebrew Dictionary*, PC Study Bible 3, copyright © 1994 Biblesoft and International Bible Translators, Inc., s.v. "*marpe*," OT:4832.
3. Ibid., s.v. "*celeph*," OT:5558.
4. Ibid., s.v., "*calaph*," OT:5557.

## Chapter 3—Seeing the Oak Tree in the Acorn

1. Gladwell, *Outliers*.
2. ThinkExist.com, "Robert H. Schuller," http://thinkexist.com/quotation/tough_times_never_last_but_tough_people/167932.html (accessed July 28, 2011).

## Chapter 4—Pursuing Purity in Heart and Mind

1. George Barna, *Revolutionary Parenting* (Carol Stream, IL: Tyndale House Publishers, Inc., 2007).
2. Donald F. Roberts et al., "Kids & Media @ the New Millennium," A Kaiser Family Foundation Report, November 1999, http://www.kff.org/entmedia/upload/Kids-Media-The-New-Millennium-Report.pdf (accessed September 20, 2011).
3. Ibid.

4. Dale Kunkel et al., "Sex on TV," A Biennial Report of the Kaiser Family Foundation, 2003, www.kff.org/entmedia/loader .cfm?url=/commonspot/security/getfile.cfm&PageID=14209 (accessed September 20, 2011).

5. Ibid.

6. Ibid.

7. A. Chandra et al., "Does Watching Sex on Television Predict Teen Pregnancy? Findings From a National Longitudinal Survey of Youth," *Pediatrics* 122, no. 5 (2008): 1047–1054, http://pediatrics.aappublications.org/content/122/5/1047.full (accessed September 20, 2011).

8. L'Engle et al., "The Mass Media Are an Important Context for Adolescents' Sexual Behavior," *Journal of Adolescent Health* 38, (2006): 86–192, http://teenmedia.unc.edu/pdf/JAH.pdf (accessed September 20, 2011).

9. Brian A. Primack et al., "Exposure to Sexual Lyrics and Sexual Experience Among Urban Adolescents," *American Journal of Preventive Medicine* 36, no. 4 (2009): 317–323, http://www.ajpmonline.org/article/S0749-3797%2808%2901011-8/abstract (accessed September 20, 2011).

10. Barna Group, "Christian Parents Are Not Comfortable With Media but Buy Them for Their Kids Anyway," http://www.barna.org/family-kids-articles/90-christian-parents-are-not-comfortable-with-media-but-buy-them-for-their-kids-anyway (accessed July 29, 2011). Permission requested.

11. Stephanie Desmon, "1 in 4 U.S. Teen Girls Infected With STD," *Baltimore Sun*, March 12, 2008, http://articles.baltimoresun.com/2008-03-12/news/0803120122_1_common-stds-transmitted-diseases-sexually-transmitted (accessed September 20, 2011).

12. Laura Sessions Stepp, "Study: Half of All Teens Have Had Oral Sex," *Washington Post*, September 16, 2005, http://www.washingtonpost.com/wp-dyn/content/article/2005/09/15/AR2005091500915.html (accessed September 20, 2011).

13. Julie Sullivan, "Teens' Use of Online Porn Can Lead to Addiction," *The Oregonian*, December 17, 2008, http://www.oregonlive.com/health/index.ssf/2008/12/teens_use_of_online_porn_can_l.html (accessed September 20, 2011).

14. "'Sexting' Overkill," Philly.com, April 6, 2009, http://articles
.philly.com/2009-04-06/news/25286780_1_sexting-nude
-photos-teens (accessed September 20, 2011).
15. Danice K. Eaton et al., "Youth Risk Behavior Surveillance—
United States, 2009," *Morbidity and Mortality Weekly Report
(MMWR)* 59, SSO5 (June 4, 2010): 1–142, http://www.cdc
.gov/mmwr/preview/mmwrhtml/ss5905a1.htm (accessed September 20, 2011).
16. Centers for Disease Control and Prevention, "HIV/AIDS
Surveillance Report" vol. 19 (2006):11, http://www.cdc
.gov/hiv/topics/surveillance/resources/reports/2006report/
pdf/2006SurveillanceReport.pdf (accessed September 20, 2011).
17. Rebekah Levine Coley, Bethany L. Medeiros, and Holly
S. Schindler, "Using Sibling Differences to Estimate Effects
of Parenting on Adolescent Sexual Risk Behaviors," *Journal
of Adolescent Health* 43, no. 2 (2008): 133–140, http://www
.jahonline.org/article/S1054-139X%2808%2900101-8/abstract
(accessed September 20, 2011); Sally Law, "Involved Dads
Lower Their Kids' Sex Risks," LiveScience.com, May 15, 2009,
http://www.livescience.com/3608-involved-dads-kids-sex-risks
.html (accessed September 20, 2011).
18. Ian Slatter, "New Study Shows Homeschoolers Excel Academically," Home School Legal Defense Association, August 10,
2009, http://www.hslda.org/docs/media/2009/200908100.asp
(accessed July 29, 2011). Used by permission.

## Chapter 6—Be Available

1. Meghan Vivo, "10 Things Teens Wish Their Parents Knew,"
Aspen Education Group, http://www.aspeneducation.com/
articles/10-things-teens-wish-their-parents-knew.htm (accessed
September 20, 2011). Permission requested.
2. Wikipedia.org, s.v. "Helicopter Parent," http://en.wikipedia.org/
wiki/Helicopter_parent (accessed September 20, 2011).
3. Stephen Covey, *The Seven Habits of Highly Effective People*
(New York: Simon & Schuster, Inc., 1989, 2004).

## Chapter 7—Destiny of the Diligent

1. Hayford, *Spirit-Filled Life Bible.*
2. Wikipedia.org, s.v. "Life is Good.," http://en.wikipedia.org/
wiki/Life_is_good (accessed September 20, 2011).
3. Gladwell, *Outliers.*

4. Ibid.

5. Christine Hassler, "I'm Not an Adultolesent," *The Huffington Post*, July 15, 2008, http://www.huffingtonpost.com/christine -hassler/im-not-an-adultolescent_b_112743.html (accessed September 19, 2011).

6. Ibid.

7. *Newsweek*, "Bringing Up Adultolescents," March 24, 2002, http://www.thedailybeast.com/newsweek/2002/03/24/bringing -up-adultolescents.html (accessed September 20, 2011). Permission requested.

8. John Piper, "A Church-Based Hope for 'Adultolescents,'" November 13, 2007, http://www.desiringgod.org/resource -library/taste-see-articles/a-church-based-hope-for-adultolescents (accessed September 20, 2011). Used by permission.

9. Ibid.

### CHAPTER 9—MODEL HUMILITY

1. BrainyQuote, "Saint Augustine Quotes," http://www .brainyquote.com/quotes/quotes/s/saintaugus148548.html (accessed October 25, 2011).

### CHAPTER 12—GROWING INTEGRITY

1. The Jesus Site, "Quotes by Topic: Integrity," http://www .jesussite.com/quotes/integrity.html (accessed September 21, 2011).

2. "Free to be Me" by Francesca Battistelli, copyright © 2008 by Word Music, LLC. All rights reserved. Used by permission.

3. "This Is the Stuff" by Francesca Battistelli, Ian Eskelin, and Tony Wood, copyright © 2010 by Designer Music Group, Inc., Honest and Popular Songs, Word Music, LLC, Songs From Exit 71, Sony/ATV Cross Keys Publishing. All rights reserved. Print license applied for.

### CHAPTER 13—TIMING IS EVERYTHING

1. Biblesoft's *New Exhaustive Strong's Numbers and Concordance With Expanded Greek-Hebrew Dictionary*, s.v. "zeman," OT:2165.

### CHAPTER 15—COMMON PARENTING TRAPS

1. Bryan Gottlieb, "The Only Child," http://www.metroparent .com/Metro-Parent/March-2011/The-Only-Child/ (accessed November 8, 2011).

FOR MORE INFORMATION VISIT:

www.katebattistelli.com